COOK'S
BIBLE

igloobooks

Published in 2014
by Igloo Books Ltd
Cottage Farm
Sywell
Northants
NN6 0BJ
www.igloobooks.com

Food photography and recipe development: PhotoCuisine UK
Front and back cover images © PhotoCuisine UK

HUN001 1114
4 6 8 10 9 7 5 3
ISBN: 978-1-78343-476-3

Printed and manufactured in China

Contents

Kitchen Equipment

All good home kitchens should be well stocked with a variety of pans, saucepans, baking equipment, utensils and knives. The most important knife in any kitchen should be a chef's knife, ideally (at least) 20 cm (8 in) in length with a balanced handle for comfort when gripped. Look for stainless steel varieties, which are sturdy and long lasting. Spend as much as you can afford when buying a chef's knife; a decent quality one will prove invaluable over time, provided it is well cared for. To go with a chef's knife, you should invest in a sharpening steel to maintain your knives. Before using your knives, sharpen them by drawing the blade from heel to tip against the steel, held at approximately a 20° angle; do this a couple of times on both sides to evenly sharpen your knife. A properly sharpened knife will be easy to use, as well as helping to prevent cuts and injuries as you will need to use less force to cut through ingredients. There are some tasks where a chef's knife is less than ideal; boning a chicken, or filleting a fish for example. To go with a chef's knife, you should aim to have a small paring knife to prepare vegetables, a flexible filleting knife to prepare fish, a boning knife for meat preparation and a serrated bread knife for slicing bread. After using knives, you should wash them as soon as possible in warm, soapy water using a soft sponge and dry them straight away to help prevent rusting.

To complement your knives, you will need a selection of various, accompanying utensils. A balloon whisk is great for whipping cream, or whisking flour into melted butter for a roux. A flexible fish slice is perfect for flipping fish, or meat in a frying pan. A decent selection of heatproof slotted spoons will make removing vegetables and pasta from hot water an easy task; they're also great for removing chips from hot oil. Along with slotted spoons, you should aim for a good selection of rubber spatulas and wooden spoons for stirring sauces and bringing together dough. When cooking meats and poultry, a meat thermometer is the most accurate way to test for doneness and removes any of the guesswork that might be involved. For testing baked goods, such as cakes, a wooden toothpick, or metal skewer will suffice. A solid pair of metal tongs will prove invaluable for handling cooked meats on the barbecue and they can also double up to pull spaghetti from hot water. For preparing vegetables, a Y-shaped peeler is ideal for speedy peeling, and to drain your cooked vegetables a large, wide colander is needed. A sharp pair of kitchen scissors will make snipping chives an easy task and will prove to be useful for a host of other kitchen tasks. For grating cheese, a box grater will make light work of it – a Microplane grater is also great for smaller tasks, such as grating nutmeg, or Parmesan for garnishes. These utensils will make preparing ingredients an easier task and make cooking a more enjoyable experience.

When it comes to saucepans, a small, medium and large saucepan are a good starting point for any kitchen. To go with these, you should aim for an extra two to three large saucepans for cooking pasta and poaching eggs - the larger, the better. Heavy-based versions are more expensive although they last for a long time when cared for properly. A couple of different-sized casserole dishes with lids are perfect for stews and braises; they should also be heatproof for use in the oven. A couple of frying pans are ideal for everyday cooking. These can be supplemented with sauté pans (which have slightly higher rims than a frying pan) and a large wok for stir-frying. An omelette, or crepe pan is versatile and a griddle pan can recreate barbecue results during the colder months. To go with your pans, a large collection of various mixing bowls is needed for tasks as varied as dressing salads to leaving bread dough to prove. Finally, when purchasing equipment for your kitchen, buying good quality pieces will help ensure longevity and good results.

Store Cupboard Essentials

Almost every recipe needs a cooking fat, whether that be oil, or butter. As a rule of thumb, you should keep a plentiful supply of cooking oil, such as vegetable, sunflower, or groundnut oil, in your cupboard, as well as olive oil. It is wise to keep in mind that olive oil burns at a lower temperature than the other oils and as such should be used in marinades and dressings rather than for frying. Oils such a groundnut and sunflower are great for shallow frying as they have a high burning temperature. A good supply of chilled margarine is crucial for avid bakers and every kitchen should have a block of unsalted and salted butter at any given time.

Another staple for any kitchen is a fresh supply of eggs; keep at least six large fresh eggs at any given time. They are quick and easy to cook, as well as being nutritious and irreplaceable in some recipes, particularly baking. Fresh milk can be used for poaching fish, as well as in choux pastry, not to mention for pouring over breakfast cereals and into hot drinks. As far as fresh produce, such as meat, goes, planning your meals ahead of time ensures that you are using ingredients at their freshest. If you can't use fresh meat, poultry, or fish when they are at their best, they can always be frozen for use at another time. In most cases, look to use fresh meats and fish within three days of purchase, always keeping them chilled in the fridge before using. Fresh fruits and vegetables have varying shelf lives; potatoes will keep for longer than lettuce when stored in a cool, dry place away from sunlight. Tomatoes and avocados are best kept at room temperature to preserve their taste and texture. For other salad ingredients, it is advisable to keep them chilled before using.

Keeping a good stock of dry store ingredients is much easier than fresh ones as they have a much longer shelf life. Canned chopped tomatoes, cartons of passata and canned beans, such as kidney and chickpeas, form a good basis on which to build your cupboard essentials. To go with canned vegetables such as these, a few different kinds of pasta are good to keep in reserve, as well as different kinds of rice, such as basmati and Arborio for risottos. Oats can be kept in an airtight container and used for breakfast porridge, or in muffins. Pulses, such as dried beans and lentils, keep for a good length of time when stored correctly away from light in a cool, dark place. They have the added bonus of being inexpensive as well. A well-stocked cupboard always includes a few varieties of flour; plain, self-raising and wholemeal should be the bare minimum, supplemented by strong bread flour, '00' flour and cornflour. For baking needs, sugars, such as caster, granulated and soft varieties, are essential, as are jars of honey and golden syrup.

Dried herbs and spices are invaluable in any pantry; they provide the taste and interest in many recipes. For herbs, the core of a good selection would include dried thyme, rosemary and oregano. You can supplement these with others, such as dried mint, or tarragon. Dried garlic and onion powder, while not preferable to their fresh versions when available, can be used in a pinch if supplies run low. When it comes to spices, the essentials include ground cumin, coriander, paprika (sweet and smoked), cayenne pepper, turmeric and curry powder (mild, or hot), as well as fragrant spices, such as cinnamon, nutmeg and clove. Mixed allspice is an important ingredient in baking, as well as in festive recipes, such as mulled wine; as such, it is always good to have on hand.

Finally, salt and pepper are two of the most important ingredients in any cupboard. Keep a plentiful stock of sea salt and whole black peppercorns; they can be poured into grinders to be used as and when necessary. Additionally, you could keep a container of flaked sea salt for sprinkling and garnishing, as well as some red, pink and white peppercorns for certain recipes.

Glossary of Terms

Al Dente: describes pasta that has been cooked to the point where it is tender while retaining a little crunch.

Baste: to preserve moisture during cooking by spooning juices, or melted butter, for example, over a piece of meat as it cooks.

Beat: mixing forcefully to incorporate ingredients together as evenly as possible.

Blanch: briefly submerging vegetables, for example, in boiling water to partially cook.

Blend: incorporating together at least two ingredients.

Boil: to bring a liquid up to a temperature where rapid bubbles form on the surface.

Braise: to cook a large, or whole piece of meat in liquid at a simmer.

Caramelise: to cook the sugars to a temperature where they start to brown and take on a distinct taste and appearance akin to caramel.

Clarify (butter): to separate the fat solids from the liquid.

Coat: to dip in an ingredient, such as breadcrumbs, in order to cover uniformly.

Cream: to beat butter, usually with sugar, until softened and so that the sugar dissolves – often a method used in baking.

Cure: preservation of meats by drying, or salting.

Cutting: breaking down larger ingredients into smaller parts. Often used in baking as a technique, along with folding, to help preserve trapped air ingredients and known as 'cutting and folding.'

Deglaze: to dissolve the juices and tastes on the base of a pan by adding a liquid to boil and thus dislodge. Often accompanied by physically scraping the base to help loosen.

Degrease: removing liquid fat, or oil from the surface of a soup, stew, or stock by using a ladle.

Dice: to cube ingredients, such as vegetables, or fruit, into small, uniform pieces.

Drizzle: often used to finish a dish, to lightly and casually pour over.

Dust: to lightly sprinkle a dry ingredient over, for example, icing sugar over a cake in order to garnish.

Fillet: to separate the flesh away from the bone of a piece of meat, or fish.

Flake: to break down into smaller, uneven pieces, often using your hands.

Flambé: to briefly ignite alcohol when added to other ingredients in order to burn away alcohol content.

Fold: a technique used, often in baking, to help incorporate and preserve trapped air in ingredients, such as beaten egg whites, or whipped cream. Often the second part of a two-step technique known as 'cutting and folding.'

Fricassee: a French method of cooking by braising in liquid, often applied to chicken, or rabbit.

Garnish: to decorate a dish just before serving for appearance and sometimes taste.

Glaze: to thinly cover with a layer, such as brushing on warmed jam, or melted butter

Grate: a technique used to shred ingredients for sprinkling, or appearance.

Gratin: a French term often used to describe a baked dish that is usually finished under a hot grill to form a crust, or promote browning.

Grill: a method of cooking under a high temperature.

Grind: to break down ingredients into smaller, more uniform parts; often applied to meats, or spices.

Julienne: to cut into very thin strips using a sharp knife, or mandolin.

Knead: to work a dough, or pastry with the palms of your hands in order to smooth out.

Lukewarm: a measurement of temperature, often quoted as being body temperature.

Marinate: a method of preparing and tenderizing meat over a period of time by using oil, citrus juice, vinegar, yoghurt, salt and, or, sugar and seasonings.

Mince: to crush and chop into very fine pieces, almost to the point of a paste

Pan fry: to cook something in hot oil, or butter in a frying pan.

Par-boil: to partially cook something in boiling water, so as to speed up its final cooking process, such as roasting, or baking.

Pare: to remove the outer most layer of skin from a piece of fruit, or vegetable.

Pinch: a unit of measurement of a dry ingredient; calculated by pinching an ingredient, such as salt, between index finger and thumb.

Pitted: fruits that have had their stone removed.

Poach: to cook an ingredient in liquid, often at a simmer.

Purée: to blend, or mash an ingredient until totally smooth, often using a food processor, or blender to do so.

Reduce: to decrease the volume of a liquid through evaporation by boiling.

Refresh: immediately placing a cooked item, such as a boiled egg, in iced water in order to stop the cooking process.

Render: using heat to turn solidified fat into liquid form, such as on a duck breast.

Sauté: to brown ingredients in hot oil.

Score: to make incisions in food, such as the skin of a fish, using a sharp knife.

Seal: briefly cooking in hot oil to promote browning and taste on a piece of meat, or poultry.

Shred: to cut into long, thin pieces.

Sift: to pass dry ingredients, such as flour, through a sieve in order to eliminate lumps.

Simmer: slowly cooking in liquid over low-medium heat at a temperature where bubbles rise gently to the surface.

Skim: removing fat and impurities from the surface of a simmering, or boiling liquid by using a ladle, or spoon.

Stew: to gently simmer smaller pieces of ingredients in a liquid, over a long period of time until tender.

Toss: using a lifting motion to combine together ingredients, such as salad and a dressing.

Truss: to securely tie a whole piece of poultry, such as a chicken, in order to help it retain shape and promote even cooking.

Whip: rapidly beating a liquid in order to incorporate air and promote thickness and volume.

Table of Measures

Temperature metric (ºC)	140ºC	150	170	180	190	200	220
Temperature imperial (F)	275F	300	325	350	375	400	425
Gas Mark	1	2	3	4	5	6	7

Volume metric (ml, litre)	55 ml	75	150	275	570	725	1 litre
Volume imperial (fl. oz, pint)	2 fl. oz	3	5 (¼ pint)	10 (½ pint)	1 pint	1 ¼	1 ¾

Measures metric (mm, cm)	3 mm	5 mm	1 cm	2.5	3	4	4.5
Measures imperial (in)	⅛ in	¼	½	1	1 ¼	1 ½	1 ¾

Weights metric (g, kg)	10 g	20	25	40	50	60	75
Weights imperial (oz, lb)	½ oz	¾	1	1 ½	2	2 ½	3

	50 g	75 g	100 g	125 g	150 g
liquids	¼ cup	⅓ cup	½ cup	½ cup	⅔ cup
flour	⅓ cup	½ cup	⅔ cup	¾ cup	1 cup
caster / granulated / Demerara sugar	¼ cup	⅓ cup	½ cup	½ cup	⅔ cup
brown sugar / Muscovado	¼ cup	½ cup	½ cup	¾ cup	¾ cup
butter	¼ cup	⅓ cup	½ cup	½ cup	⅔ cup
sultanas / raisins /sun-dried tomatoes	¼ cup	⅓ cup	½ cup	⅔ cup	¾ cup
currants / chocolate chips	⅓ cup	½ cup	⅔ cup	¾ cup	1 cup
ground almonds	½ cup	¾ cup	1 cup	1 ¼ cups	1 ½ cups
golden syrup / honey	¼ cup	¼ cup	⅓ cup	⅓ cup	½ cup
uncooked rice	¼ cup	⅓ cup	½ cup	⅔ cup	¾ cup
icing sugar / cocoa / grated cheese	½ cup	¾ cup	1 cup	1 ¼ cups	1 ½ cups
oats / parmesan / desiccated coconut	½ cup	¾ cup	1 cup	1 ¼ cups	1 ½ cups
fresh breadcrumbs / flaked almonds	⅔ cup	1 cup	1 ⅓ cup	1 ⅔ cups	2 cups
panko breadcrumbs	⅓ cup	½ cup	⅔ cup	¾ cup	1 cup
couscous / cooked rice	¼ cup	½ cup	½ cup	¾ cup	¾ cup
chopped nuts / grated vegetables	½ cup	⅔ cup	¾ cup	1 cup	1 ¼ cups
berries / olives / peas	⅓ cup	½ cup	⅔ cup	¾ cup	1 cup

230	240
450	475
8	9

Keeping measurements and weights as accurate as possible will help you prepare the perfect meal. As a rule, never mix imperial and metric measures in the same recipe. For example, if you are baking a cake and measure out your flour in grams, then you must also measure out your sugar and other weighted ingredients in grams.

1.2	1.5	2.25
2	2 ½	4

5	6	7.5	10	13	15	16	18	20	23	25.5	28	30
2	2 ½	3	4	5	6	6 ½	7	8	9	10	11	12

110	125	150	175	200	225	250	275	350	450	700	900	1.35 kg
4	4 ½	5	6	7	8	9	10	12	1 lb	1 lb 8 oz	2	3

175 g	200 g	225 g	250 g	300 g	350 g	400 g	450 g	500 g	900 g	1 kg
⅔ cup	¾ cup	¾ cup	1 cup	1 ¼ cups	1 ½ cups	1 ⅔ cups	1 ¾ cups	2 cups	3 ½ cups	4 cups
1 ¼ cups	1 ⅓ cups	1 ½ cups	1 ⅔ cups	2 cups	2 ⅓ cups	2 ⅔ cups	3 cups	3 ⅓ cups	6 cups	7 cups
¾ cup	¾ cup	1 cup	1 ¼ cups	1 ⅓ cups	1 ½ cups	1 ¾ cups	2 cups	2 ¼ cups	4 cups	4 ½ cups
1 cup	1 ¼ cups	1 ⅓ cups	1 ½ cups	1 ¾ cups	2 cups	2 ⅓ cups	2 ½ cups	2 ¾ cups	5 cups	5 ¾ cups
¾ cup	¾ cup	1 cup	1 ¼ cups	1 ⅓ cups	1 ½ cups	1 ¾ cups	2 cups	2 ¼ cups	4 cups	4 ½ cups
¾ cup	1 cup	1 ¼ cups	1 ¼ cups	1 ½ cups	1 ¾ cups	2 cups	2 ¼ cups	2 ½ cups	4 ½ cups	5 cups
1 ¼ cups	1 ⅓ cups	1 ½ cups	1 ⅔ cups	2 cups	2 ⅓ cups	2 ⅔ cups	3 cups	3 ⅓ cups	6 cups	7 cups
1 ¾ cups	2 cups	2 ¼ cups	2 ½ cups	3 cups	3 ½ cups	4 cups	4 ½ cups	5 cups	9 cups	10 cups
½ cup	⅔ cup	⅔ cup	¾ cup	¾ cup	1 cup	1 ¼ cups	1 ¼ cups	1 ½ cups	2 ½ cups	2 ¾ cups
¾ cup	1 cup	1 ¼ cups	1 ¼ cups	1 ½ cups	1 ¾ cups	2 cups	2 ¼ cups	2 ½ cups	4 ½ cups	5 cups
1 ¾ cups	2 cups	2 ¼ cups	2 ½ cups	3 cups	3 ½ cups	4 cups	4 ½ cups	5 cups	9 cups	10 cups
1 ¾ cups	2 cups	2 ¼ cups	2 ½ cups	3 cups	3 ½ cups	4 cups	4 ½ cups	5 cups	9 cups	10 cups
2 ⅓ cups	2 ⅔ cups	3 cups	3 ⅓ cups	4 cups	4 ⅔ cups	5 ⅓ cups	6 cups	6 ⅔ cups	12 cups	13 ⅓ cups
1 ¼ cups	1 ⅓ cups	1 ½ cups	1 ⅔ cups	2 cups	2 ⅓ cups	2 ⅔ cups	3 cups	3 ⅓ cups	6 cups	7 cups
1 cup	1 ¼ cups	1 ⅓ cups	1 ½ cups	1 ¾ cups	2 cups	2 ⅓ cups	2 ½ cups	2 ¾ cups	5 cups	5 ¾ cups
1 ½ cups	1 ⅔ cups	1 ¾ cups	2 cups	2 ½ cups	2 ¾ cups	3 ¼ cups	3 ⅔ cups	4 cups	7 ¼ cups	8 cups
1 ¼ cups	1 ⅓ cups	1 ½ cups	1 ⅔ cups	2 cups	2 ⅓ cups	2 ⅔ cups	3 cups	3 ⅓ cups	6 cups	7 cups

EGGS

Freshness of Eggs

Cooking with fresh eggs produces the best results. Where possible, try and use the freshest eggs available, particularly when baking, or serving eggs poached, fried, or scrambled. You can easily test for the freshness of an egg by carefully lowering it into a jug of cold water. If the egg is fresh, it will sink to the bottom, staying horizontal. If the egg is tilted diagonally towards vertical it could be up to one week old. If it sits vertical with the tip pointing up, it is stale.

Boiling Eggs

There are two main ways to boil an egg. For the first method, place an egg in a saucepan and cover with cold water. Bring the water to the boil over a moderate heat and once the water starts to boil, cook for 10 minutes precisely. For a soft-boiled egg, cook the egg for 7–8 minutes.

The second method involves bringing a saucepan of water to the boil over a moderate heat before gently lowering the egg into the water. Cook for 12 minutes for a hard-boiled egg and 9–10 minutes for a soft-boiled one. With both methods, it is important to run the eggs under cold, running water once cooked in order to stop the cooking process. Once cool, you can lightly tap the eggs against a hard surface to crack the shell before peeling.

Poaching Eggs

As with boiling, there are a few methods when it comes to poaching eggs. Here, we will outline three main methods to help you poach an egg with a perfectly set white and a runny yolk. With all three methods, it is advisable to use a timer to help prevent overcooking your eggs.

For the first method, bring a deep saucepan of water to a steady simmer; it is important that the saucepan is deep in order to let the egg drop into the water without touching the bottom and catching. Add 1 tbsp of white wine vinegar to the water and stir briefly. Crack an egg into a small cup and gently slide it into the middle of the simmering water. Watching carefully, poach the egg for 3 minutes, making sure that the water never exceeds its steady simmer. After 3 minutes, the white should be set around the yolk, at which point you can carefully remove it from the water using a slotted spoon. Drain the egg on kitchen paper; trim any straggly pieces of white, if desired, before serving.

For the second method, add enough water to a small frying pan so that it reaches about 4 cm in depth. Bring the water to a gentle simmer before cracking the egg directly into the water; cook for 3 minutes until the white and yolk are set. As with the first method, you can crack the egg into a small cup before pouring into the water if that is easier.

In the third and final method, fill a deep saucepan with water and bring to a simmer. Crack an egg into a cup and set it to one side. Take a whisk and firmly stir the water to create a whirlpool in the water. With the water still swirling, carefully slide the egg into the middle and cook for 3 minutes. Remove with a slotted spoon and drain on kitchen paper before serving.

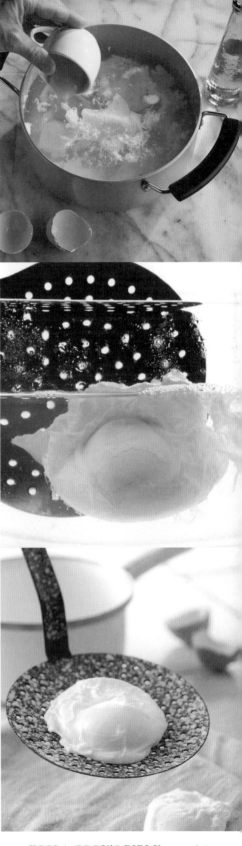

Scrambling Eggs

Scrambled eggs can be a quick and satisfying breakfast accompaniment when prepared properly. The first method for scrambling eggs is perhaps the quickest and simplest method. Heat a small knob of butter in a heavy-based saucepan or frying pan set over a moderate heat. Beat together a couple of eggs with a pinch of salt and pepper. Once the butter stops foaming, add the beaten egg and stir continuously until almost, but not entirely, set. Remove the pan from the heat and let the residual heat finish cooking them before serving immediately.

The second method is more time consuming, but produces a more luxurious version. Crack a couple of eggs into a cold pan set over a very low heat. Add a couple of knobs of butter and cook the eggs, stirring frequently, until they start to set; 6–7 minutes. Just before the eggs are completely set, add another knob of butter and remove the pan from the heat, allowing the residual heat to finish cooking them. Adjust the seasoning to taste before serving.

The third method calls for the addition of a little milk or cream. Whisk a couple of eggs together in a jug with a couple of tablespoons of either whole milk or single cream and a generous pinch of salt and pepper. Heat a small knob of butter in a frying or saucepan set over a medium heat. Once melted, add the egg mixture and leave them untouched for 30 seconds. Using a spatula, start to fold the eggs over themselves, rather than stirring them. Continue to fold and cook until softly set at which point they can be served.

Basic Omelette

Making a perfect omelette can be tricky without appropriate instruction. By following this guideline, you should be able to produce good results from the first go.

Roughly whisk together a couple of eggs in a small bowl with one tablespoon of cold water and a pinch of salt and pepper. Heat a knob of butter in an omelette or small frying pan set over a moderate heat. As soon as the butter stops foaming, add the beaten egg mixture to the pan. Start to tilt the pan to let the egg cover the entire surface. Once the egg starts to set, draw in the edges towards the middle to create space for the uncooked egg to run to as you tilt the pan. Just before the egg is totally set, fold the sides inwards over the middle, overlapping to create your omelette. Slide the omelette out of the pan onto a serving plate and serve immediately.

Frying Eggs

Frying an egg is quick and simple. Just add a tablespoon of vegetable or sunflower oil to a small frying pan and set over a moderate heat. Once the oil starts to shimmer crack an egg directly into it; take care as the egg can spit and crackle at this point. Reduce the heat a little and let the white set; once set and the edges are starting to colour, carefully flip the egg with a spatula to cook the other side briefly should you wish for it 'sunny side down.' If not, cover the pan with a lid for about 1 minute to help briefly set the yolk; it will still be runny. Serve immediately for best results.

Coddling Eggs

When coddling eggs, using a coddler will produce the best results. If not, you can always use a ramekin instead. Lightly butter the insides of a few coddlers or ramekins before cracking eggs directly into them. Cover the eggs with milk before adding a pinch of seasoning on top. Carefully place in an empty roasting tin; carefully pour boiling water into the tin and around the coddlers, or ramekins so that it reaches halfway up their exteriors. Cook in a moderately hot oven for 4–5 minutes until the whites are set.

Separating Eggs

An effective, if untidy, method for separating an egg is by using your bare hands. Ready two empty bowls to one side. Give the egg a firm, yet gentle tap on its side against a hard work surface to create a crack. Once cracked, carefully pull apart the two parts of the egg, letting some of the white run into one bowl. Pour the remaining white and yolk into one hand, letting the white run through slightly split fingers into the egg white bowl. Drop the egg yolk carefully into the other bowl.

Another method for separating an egg is quite similar; instead of using your hands to separate the white from the yolk, use the two pieces of shell to help separate away the white from the yolk. After cracking the egg, carefully tip the egg white and yolk between the two shells, letting the white flow out into a bowl beneath. Once all the white as been removed, drop the yolk into another bowl.

Egg White Omelette

Making an egg white omelette is not unlike making a regular omelette; whisk together two egg whites with a half-tablespoon of water and a pinch of salt and pepper until frothy. Heat a small knob of butter in an omelette, or small frying pan, which is set over a moderate heat. Once it stops frothing, add the egg white mixture to the pan and tilt the pan, to help the mixture coat the surface. Once the white starts to set, lift the edges up to let the uncooked white run underneath and set. Just before the omelette is completely set, fold the edges inwards, overlapped, to make your omelette. Slide carefully out of the pan and onto a serving plate.

INGREDIENTS

4 medium eggs
2 tsp Dijon mustard
2 tbsp white wine vinegar
100 ml / 3 ½ fl. oz / ½ cup sunflower oil
350 g / 12 oz / 3 cups green (string) beans
2 little gem lettuce, leaves separated
100 g / 3 ½ oz / ¼ cup walnuts, roughly
    chopped
a small bunch of chive stalks, finely chopped
salt and freshly ground black pepper

Egg, Green Beans and Walnut Salad

1. Cook the eggs in a saucepan of boiling water for 10 minutes before draining and refreshing in iced water.

2. Whisk together the mustard, vinegar and a little seasoning in a small mixing bowl until smooth.

3. Add the sunflower oil in a slow, steady stream, whisking constantly until a thickened dressing comes together; cover and set to one side.

4. Cook the green beans in a saucepan of salted, boiling water for 3 minutes until tender; drain and run under cold water.

5. Drain the eggs before peeling and halving.

6. Toss together the green beans, gem lettuce, walnuts, chives and egg halves with the dressing.

7. Serve on a large platter.

SERVES: **4**

PREPARATION TIME: **10–15 MINUTES**

COOKING TIME: **6 MINUTES**

INGREDIENTS

110 g / 4 oz / ½ cup Greek yoghurt
75 g / 3 oz / ⅓ cup mayonnaise
½ tsp dried dill
a few sprigs of chive, finely chopped
1 tbsp white wine vinegar
8 small eggs
4 English muffins, split
75 g / 3 oz / 1 ½ cups baby spinach leaves,
    washed and dried
salt and freshly ground black pepper

Poached Egg and Spinach Muffin

1. Beat together the Greek yoghurt, mayonnaise, dried dill, chives and seasoning in a small mixing bowl.

2. Bring a large saucepan of water to a steady simmer, then stir in the white wine vinegar.

3. Crack four eggs into separate cups and slide carefully into the water, poaching for exactly 3 minutes.

4. Remove with a slotted spoon and drain on kitchen paper. Keep warm to one side as you poach the other four.

5. Meanwhile, toast the muffin halves in a toaster, or under a hot grill.

6. Spread with the yoghurt and mayonnaise and top half with some spinach leaves.

7. Arrange on plates and sit the other muffin halves on top and sit the poached eggs on top.

8. Serve immediately.

SERVES: **4**

PREPARATION TIME: **10 MINUTES**

COOKING TIME: **10 MINUTES**

INGREDIENTS

4 slices of sourdough bread
8 large eggs
20 button mushrooms
75 ml / 3 fl. oz / ⅓ cup whole milk
a few chive stalks, finely chopped
a few sprigs of tarragon, finely chopped
55 g / 2 oz / ¼ cup cold butter, cubed
salt and freshly ground black pepper

Scrambled Eggs and Mushrooms

1. Preheat the grill to hot, then toast the slices of sourdough on both sides until lightly golden.

2. Whisk the eggs with the milk, chives, half of the chopped tarragon, half of the cubed butter and some seasoning.

3. Melt the remaining butter in a large frying pan over a moderate heat until the butter stops foaming.

4. Sauté the mushrooms with seasoning and the remaining tarragon until golden-brown and tender.

5. Scramble the eggs in a hot saucepan set over a medium heat, stirring frequently until just cooked through and shiny in appearance.

6. Adjust the seasoning to taste and spoon on top of the toast, placing them on plates.

7. Spoon over the mushrooms and serve immediately.

INGREDIENTS

700 g / 1 lb 9 oz / 4 ⅔ cups floury
  potatoes, peeled and cut into 1 cm
  (½ in) cubes
2 tbsp olive oil
1 onion, finely chopped
1 clove of garlic, minced
6 large eggs, beaten
175 ml / 6 fl. oz / ¼ cup whole milk
a pinch of paprika
a small bunch of flat-leaf parsley, finely
  chopped
150 g / 5 oz / 1 cup vine tomatoes,
  chopped
salt and freshly ground black pepper

Spanish Potato Tortilla

1. Preheat the oven to 180°C (160°C fan) / 350F / gas 4.

2. Cook the potatoes in a large saucepan of salted, boiling water for 6–7 minutes until tender; drain and leave to cool.

3. Heat the oil in a large, ovenproof sauté pan set over a medium heat.

4. Sauté the onion and garlic with a little seasoning for 3–4 minutes until softened, then add the potato.

5. Continue to cook for a few minutes, then remove the vegetables to a plate.

6. Whisk together the eggs, milk, paprika, parsley and seasoning in a jug, then add half to the pan and set over a low heat.

7. Spoon over half of the vegetable mixture, then top with the tomatoes and then the rest of the vegetables.

8. Leave to cook, untouched, until the base is just set, then pour in the remaining egg mixture.

9. Transfer to the oven to cook for 8–10 minutes until set and golden in appearance.

10. Remove from the oven and turn out before slicing and serving.

MAKES: **8**

PREPARATION TIME: **15 MINUTES**

COOKING TIME: **1 ½–¾ HOURS**

INGREDIENTS

4 medium egg whites, at room
   temperature
a pinch of salt
225 g / 8 oz / 1 cup caster (superfine)
   sugar
2 tbsp demerara sugar

Meringues Coated in Brown Sugar

1. Preheat the oven to 110°C (90°C fan) / 225F / gas ¼ and line two large baking trays with greaseproof paper.

2. Using an electric hand-held whisk, whisk the eggs whites with a pinch of salt in a large, clean mixing bowl until stiffly peaked.

3. Add the caster sugar, one tablespoon at a time, as you continue to whisk the mixture. Make sure to beat the mixture well between additions.

4. Once the meringue mixture is thick and glossy, spoon into a piping bag fitted with a large star-shaped nozzle.

5. Pipe 8 large swirls onto the baking trays, spaced apart.

6. Bake for 1 ½–¾ hours until crisp and set.

7. Leave to cool on a wire rack, sprinkled with demerara sugar on top.

SERVES: **4**

PREPARATION TIME: **25 MINUTES**

COOKING TIME: **12–15 MINUTES**

INGREDIENTS

55 g / 2 oz / ¼ cup unsalted butter,
  softened
2 tbsp plain (all purpose) flour, plus
  extra for dusting
300 ml / 10 ½ fl. oz / 1 ¼ cup whole
  milk
4 large eggs, separated
1 tsp Dijon mustard
75 g / 3 oz / ⅓ cup Cheddar, grated
55 g / 2 oz / ½ cup Comté or Gruyère,
  grated
salt and pepper

Cheese Soufflé

1. Preheat the oven to 200°C (180°C fan) / 400°F / gas 6.

2. Brush the insides of 4 individual, ceramic ramekins with half of the softened butter using a pastry brush, making upwards strokes as you do. Chill for 10 minutes.

3. Melt the rest of the butter in a saucepan over a medium heat, and then whisk in the flour until you have a smooth roux.

4. Cook the roux for 1–2 minutes, whisking occasionally, until blonde in appearance.

5. Whisk in the milk in a slow, steady stream until you have a thickened sauce, then whisk in the egg yolks, mustard and grated cheeses.

6. Simmer the sauce for 6–7 minutes over a low heat, adjusting the seasoning as necessary, then set to one side.

7. Whisk the egg whites in a clean mixing bowl with a pinch of salt until softly peaked.

8. Whisk a third of the whites into the cheese sauce, and then fold in the remaining egg whites using a cutting and folding technique.

9. Spoon into the ramekins and run the tip of your finger around the insides of the rim. Transfer to a baking tray.

10. Bake for 12–15 minutes until golden and risen.

11. Remove from the oven and serve immediately with a dusting of flour on top.

POTATOES

Types of Potato

Most potatoes fall into two distinct categories – floury and waxy. Both kinds have their uses in the kitchen, with floury potatoes preferred for mashed potatoes and chips because their dry, fluffy textures tend to produce better results. Examples of floury potatoes are King Edward, Desiree and Rooster. Waxy potatoes are preferable when making dishes such as potato salad because they hold their shape better when cooked. Examples of waxy potatoes are Anya, Charlotte and Pink Fir Apple.

There are certain varieties of potato that can be used as all-rounders. These potatoes can be used in a variety of ways, whether that be mashing, frying, chipping, or boiling. The best example of this kind of potato is a Maris Piper. Maris Piper is an extremely versatile variety of potato and is often a good standby for your kitchen cupboard when you need a potato that can be turned into mash, chips, or even roasted. Remember to store your potatoes in a clean, dry, dark environment away from moisture and direct sunlight, so they don't spoil.

Boiled Potatoes

When boiling potatoes, the most important thing to remember is that the potatoes should be diced evenly to help even cooking. Peel (if desired) the potatoes and cut into even chunks. Place in a large saucepan and cover with cold water. Add a pinch of salt and boil the water over a moderate heat. Boil the potatoes steadily for 18–22 minutes until tender. Drain well and leave to steam-dry for a few minutes before serving.

Mashed Potatoes

As with roast potatoes, Maris Pipers are a great choice for mashed potato. Desiree, or King Edwards would also be a suitable choice. Peel (if desired) 1 kg / 2 lb 4 oz / 6 cups of potatoes and cut into even chunks. Place in a large saucepan and cover with cold water. Add a pinch of salt and boil the water over a moderate heat. Cook the potatoes at a steady boil for 18–22 minutes until tender. Drain well and leave to steam-dry for a few minutes before returning to a clean saucepan. Add 75 g / 3 oz / 1/3 cup softened butter and mash well with a potato masher. If you have a ricer, pass the potatoes through it into a clean saucepan before adding the butter. Add 75 ml / 3 fl. oz / 1/3 cup whole milk, or single cream and mash again until velvety and smooth. Adjust the seasoning to taste before serving.

Roast Potatoes

Roast potatoes can be the perfect accompaniment to dishes, such as roast chicken or beef. For the best results, use approximately 1 kg / 2 lb 4 oz / 6 cups of Maris Piper potatoes; preheat the oven to 200°C (180°C fan) / 400F / gas 6. Peel and dice the potatoes into even chunks before par-boiling in a saucepan of salted, boiling water for 10 minutes until tender. As the potatoes are cooking, put 110 g / 4 oz / ½ cup duck, or goose fat into a roasting tray and place in the oven to get hot. Drain the potatoes in a colander before covering with a plate or lid and shaking vigorously to rough up their edges. Sprinkle a tablespoon of plain flour over them before shaking again briefly to coat. Carefully add them to the hot fat in the roasting tray; it will be very hot, so use oven mitts when moving the tray, as well as keeping a safe distance when adding the potatoes. Roast the potatoes for 20 minutes before removing and turning them over. Return to the oven for another 20–25 minutes until they are golden and crisp. Season the roast potatoes with a little salt before serving.

Jacket Potatoes

When baking jacket potatoes, try and select evenly sized potatoes, approximately 225 g / 8 oz in weight, to ensure even cooking times. Wash and dry the potatoes thoroughly before pricking their skins with a fork a few times. Rub with a little olive oil before massaging a little flaked sea salt into the skins. Cook them in an oven preheated to 190°C (170°C fan) / 375F / gas 5 for 1 ¾–2 hours until the skin is crisp and the flesh is tender and fluffy – the potatoes can be placed directly onto clean racks without needing to use a baking tray. Leave the potatoes to cool briefly before serving, ideally with butter, flaked sea salt and cracked black pepper.

Pan-fried Potatoes

The key to pan-fried potatoes is par-boiling them before frying to ensure a soft interior to go with a golden, crisp exterior. You can use either floury, or waxy potatoes when pan-frying; Charlotte potatoes work particularly well with this method. Par-boil the potatoes for 15–18 minutes until their insides are tender before draining well and leaving to steam dry. Cut larger potatoes in half before melting a generous knob of butter with a tablespoon of sunflower oil in a large frying, or sauté pan. Add the potatoes and let them cook, untouched, over a moderate heat for 2 minutes before reducing the heat to medium. Continue to cook for a further 8–10 minutes, turning occasionally, until golden and crisp and season generously before serving.

Chips

Making chips from scratch may seem daunting, but in practice all it requires is the proper equipment. Having a deep-fat fryer makes the process easy, but chips can still be made without one. A cooking thermometer is essential, however.

Start by scrubbing clean some floury potatoes, such as Roosters or Maris Pipers; aim for approximately 200 g / 7 oz / 1 ⅓ cups raw potatoes per portion. You can leave the potatoes unpeeled for a more rustic style of chip. Cut the potatoes into 1 cm (½ in) thick chip shapes and rinse them under cold running water to get rid of excess starch; drain well. Place in a saucepan of salted water before bringing to the boil. Once boiling, reduce to a simmer and cook until just tender to the point of a knife. Drain the par-boiled chips before chilling.

Meanwhile, heat at least 1 l / 1 pint 16 fl. oz / 4 cups of vegetable oil in a deep-fat fryer, or heavy-based saucepan to 120°C / 250F. A deep-fat fryer should have a temperature gauge that can be set. If you are using a thermometer and a heavy-based saucepan, bring the oil up to temperature and adjust the heat settings beneath the pan to keep the oil at a constant temperature. Blanch the cooled chips in the oil for 5 minutes, working in batches so as to not overcrowd them. Drain the blanched chips and carefully pat dry before chilling again.

Just before serving, increase the temperature of the oil to 170°C / 340F. Fry the chips, in batches, until golden and crisp. Drain well, season, and serve immediately for best results.

Sautéed Potatoes

Sautéed potatoes are an elegant alternative to the rustic style of pan-fried potatoes. Using floury or waxy potatoes, par-boil them for 15–18 minutes until the flesh is tender. Drain well and leave to cool until the potatoes are easy enough to handle before cutting into 1 cm (½ in) thick slices. Melt a generous knob of butter with a tablespoon of olive, or sunflower oil in a large sauté pan set over a moderate heat. Add the sliced potatoes, in an even layer, and let them brown in the oil and butter before flipping to brown the other side. Add a little seasoning before draining on kitchen paper and serving.

Wedges

As with chips, it is best to pick a floury potato when making wedges. Preheat the oven to 190°C (170°C fan) / 375F / gas 5. Using 200 g / 7 oz / 1 ⅓ cups potatoes per person, scrub the potatoes well before drying and cutting into wedges. Rinse the cut potatoes under cold running water before par-boiling in a saucepan of salted, boiling water for 10 minutes. Drain well and dry thoroughly before tossing with a tablespoon of oil (per portion) and a generous sprinkling of salt and pepper. Arrange on a large baking tray, or in a roasting tin before transferring to the oven to bake for 40–45 minutes, turning halfway through, until they are golden on the outside and fluffy within.

SERVES: **4**

PREPARATION TIME: **15 MINUTES**

COOKING TIME: **11–15 MINUTES**

INGREDIENTS

1 kg / 2 lb / 6 ⅔ cups Desiree potatoes, peeled
1 onion, finely chopped
a small bunch of flat-leaf parsley, roughly chopped
2 tbsp sunflower oil
2 tbsp unsalted butter
a small handful of rocket (arugula)
salt and freshly ground black pepper

Stacked Potato Rostis

1. Preheat the oven to 140°C (120°C fan) / 275F / gas 1.

2. Roughly grate the potatoes and dry really well using a clean tea towel.

3. Once dried, place in a bowl and add the onion, parsley and seasoning.

4. Heat together half the oil and butter in a large frying pan set over a medium heat.

5. Drop generous tablespoons of the potato mixture into the pan, placed in mounds and spaced apart.

6. Gently flatten the mounds using a spatula or fish slice and then cook for 6–8 minutes until browned underneath.

7. Flip the rostis and cook the other side for 5–7 minutes until lightly browned.

8. Remove to a plate lined with greaseproof paper and keep warm in the oven.

9. Add the remaining butter and oil to the pan and cook the remaining potato mixture in the same fashion.

10. Serve the rostis in stacks with a rocket leaf garnish on top.

SERVES: **4**

PREPARATION TIME: **30 MINUTES**

COOKING TIME: **10 MINUTES**

INGREDIENTS

2 x 350 g / 12 oz baking potatoes, scrubbed
   clean
350 g / 12 oz / 2 ⅓ cups plain (all purpose)
   flour, plus extra for kneading
2 tbsp olive oil
250 g / 9 oz / 1 ⅔ cups yellow cherry
   tomatoes, some halved
150 g / 5 oz / 1 cup cherry tomatoes,
   quartered
200 g / 7 oz / 2 cups mozzarella balls, drained
a small bunch of basil, chopped
55 g / 2 oz / 1 cup rocket (arugula)
salt and freshly ground black pepper

Tricolore Gnocchi

1. Boil the potatoes whole and unpeeled in salted water until easily pierced by a fork; drain and leave to cool until slightly warm.

2. Peel the skins and use an electric hand whisk to beat the potato flesh until smooth.

3. Stir in the flour and 1 tsp of salt mixing well until combined.

4. Knead this mixture on a lightly floured surface until no longer sticky; add a little extra flour if needed so that you have a smooth dough.

5. Take care not to overwork the dough – this stage should take 4–5 minutes.

6. Divide the dough into 4 and roll into long sausages roughly 3 cm (1 ⅓ in) in diameter.

7. Cut the sausages into small chunks and roll each piece off a fork to create indentations in the gnocchi; arrange on a floured tray until ready to cook.

8. Bring a large pan of salted water to the boil and cook the gnocchi for 4–5 minutes, or until they rise to the

surface; remove to a tray lined with kitchen paper to drain.

9. Heat the olive oil in a large sauté pan set over a moderate heat; add the gnocchi and pan-fry for 2 minutes before adding the tomatoes and seasoning.

10. Cook for 30 seconds before stirring through the mozzarella balls and basil.

11. Serve in bowls garnished with rocket leaves.

SERVES: **4**

PREPARATION TIME: **10 MINUTES**

COOKING TIME: **15–20 MINUTES**

INGREDIENTS

1 kg / 2 lb 4 oz / 6 ⅔ cups new potatoes
1 large shallot, finely chopped
75 ml / 3 fl. oz / ⅓ cup extra-virgin olive oil
½ lemon, juiced
a small bunch of flat-leaf parsley, finely
   chopped
a small bunch of chervil, finely chopped
salt and freshly ground black pepper

Potato Salad

1. Cook the potatoes in a large
   saucepan of salted, boiling water
   for 15–20 minutes, until tender.

2. Drain and leave to cool before
   cutting larger potatoes in half.

3. Place in a bowl and add the
   shallot, olive oil, lemon juice,
   parsley, chervil and seasoning.

4. Stir well to combine
   serve warm or cold.

SERVES: **4**

PREPARATION TIME: **5–10 MINUTES**

COOKING TIME: **1 ½–2 HOURS**

INGREDIENTS

4 x 225 g / 8 oz baking potatoes, scrubbed
   clean
2 tbsp olive oil
a small bunch of coriander (cilantro)
225 g / 8 oz / 1 cup sour cream
salt and freshly ground black pepper

Baked Potato with Cream and Herbs

1. Preheat the oven to 190°C (170°C fan) / 375F / gas 5.

2. Prick the potatoes with a fork before rubbing with olive oil.

3. Season with salt, then bake in the oven for 1 ½–2 hours until the skin is crisp and the flesh is soft.

4. Remove from the oven and leave to cool for a few minutes.

5. Meanwhile, finely chop most of the coriander, then stir into the sour cream in a small mixing bowl.

6. Cut the baked potatoes in half, spooning the sour cream mixture into them.

7. Garnish with the remaining coriander before serving.

SERVES: **4**

PREPARATION TIME: **15 MINUTES**

COOKING TIME: **40–50 MINUTES**

INGREDIENTS

1 kg / 2 lb 4 oz / 6 ⅔ cups Charlotte
  potatoes
75 ml / 3 fl. oz / ⅓ cup olive oil
8–10 fresh bay leaves
1 tbsp flaked sea salt

Whole Roast Potatoes

1. Preheat the oven to 190°C (170°C fan) / 375F / gas 5.

2. Parboil the potatoes in a large saucepan of salted, boiling water for 12–15 minutes, until just tender.

3. Drain and leave to steam dry for 5 minutes.

4. Toss in a roasting tin with the olive oil, bay leaves and half of the salt.

5. Roast for 40–50 minutes until the skins are golden and crisp.

6. Serve fresh from the oven with the remaining flaked sea salt scattered over them.

SERVES: **4**

PREPARATION TIME: **20 MINUTES**

COOKING TIME: **15–18 MINUTES**

INGREDIENTS

1 kg / 2 lb 4 oz / 6 ⅔ cups floury potatoes,
  peeled and evenly diced
110 ml / 4 fl. oz / ½ cup extra-virgin
  olive oil
½ shallot, finely chopped
a small bunch of chive stalks, finely chopped
75 g / 3 oz / ⅔ cup hazelnuts (cobnuts),
  roughly chopped
salt and freshly ground black pepper

Hazelnut Mashed Potatoes

1. Cook the potatoes in a large saucepan of salted, boiling water for 15–20 minutes, until tender.

2. Drain and leave to steam dry for a few minutes, then add three-quarters of the oil. Mash until smooth.

3. Add the chopped chives, shallot and seasoning and mash again briefly.

4. Stir through the nuts before spooning into bowls.

5. Drizzle with the remaining olive oil before serving.

SERVES: **4**

PREPARATION TIME: **20–25 MINUTES**

COOKING TIME: **6–8 MINUTES**

INGREDIENTS

750 g / 1 lb 10 oz / 5 cups new potatoes
2 tbsp sunflower oil
1 tbsp unsalted butter
a small bunch of oregano
coarse sea salt and freshly ground black
    pepper

Sautéed Potatoes with Sea Salt

1. Cook the potatoes in a large saucepan of salted, boiling water for 15–20 minutes, until tender.

2. Drain and leave to steam dry for a few minutes. Finely chop some of the oregano and set to one side.

3. Heat together the oil and butter in a large sauté pan set over a moderate heat.

4. Add the potatoes and sauté for 6–8 minutes, turning occasionally, until golden.

5. Stir through the chopped oregano and season with coarse sea salt and pepper.

6. Serve from the pan, garnished with the remaining oregano on top.

SERVES: **6**

PREPARATION TIME: **15–20 MINUTES**

COOKING TIME: **1 HOUR 15 MINUTES**

INGREDIENTS

1 tbsp unsalted butter, softened
325 ml / 11 fl. oz / 1 ⅓ cups whole milk
325 ml / 11 fl. oz / 1 ⅓ cups double (heavy)
  cream
2 cloves of garlic, peeled and halved
2 sprigs of thyme
1.75 kg / 4 lb / 12 cups floury potatoes, peeled
110 g / 4 oz / 1 cup Gruyère, grated
a few bay leaves, to garnish
salt and freshly ground black pepper

Gratin Dauphinoise

1. Preheat the oven to 180°C (160°C fan) / 350F / gas 4.

2. Grease a large rectangular baking dish with the butter and set to one side.

3. Combine the milk, cream, garlic and thyme in a saucepan. Bring to a simmer over a moderate heat, then remove from the heat and strain into a jug.

4. Thinly slice the potatoes, pat them dry and layer in the baking dish, seasoning between the layers.

5. Pour the milk and cream mixture over them and cover the dish with foil and bake for 55–60 minutes, until the potatoes are tender.

6. Remove from the oven, discard the foil and top with the Gruyère.

7. Return to the oven for 10–15 minutes to melt the cheese.

8. Remove the dish from the oven and let it sit for 5 minutes before serving, garnished with bay leaves.

PASTA

Types of Pasta

Pasta is the perfect standby in any kitchen as it is quick and easy to prepare, as well as being cheap and nutritious. Most pasta is sold in dried form, but it can also be purchased fresh for a richer, more authentic dish. Despite the ease of buying and preparing dried, or fresh pasta from the supermarket, it is relatively easy to prepare at home. If you are interested in preparing fresh pasta at home, you should invest in a good quality pasta maker – this will remove a lot of the hassle when trying to roll out your pasta, thus making the process effortless, as well as producing better results.

Different pasta shapes have different applications in certain dishes. Shapes such as Rigatoni, Penne and Conchiglie are ideal for thicker, meat-based sauces, such as Bolognaise. Their holes are good at catching and allowing sauce to cling to them. Shapes such as Spaghetti, Linguine and Tagliatelle are ideal for fluid, creamy sauces, such as Carbonara, where the sauce can stick to the full length of each strand. By matching the pasta shape to the sauce, you guarantee that each forkful will contain a good ratio of pasta to sauce.

In addition to these well-known shapes are more exotic types of pasta. Shapes such as Ditalini, Orecchiette and elbow Macaroni are great added to soups. Squid ink is added to pasta dough to produce a dark, exotic style of pasta that pairs particularly well with seafood. There are varieties of fusilli that have spinach and sun-dried tomato added to produce vivid presentation and taste.

A particular Italian specialty is filled pasta; Ravioli, Tortellini and Agnelotti are all prime examples of filled pastas. Nowadays it is easy enough to purchase filled pastas in shops, but there is a certain kind of satisfaction to be gained from making it fresh at home. Fillings can be meat, fish, or vegetable based, and soft cheese is often used to fill pasta as well. A particular advantage of making your own filled pasta at home is the freedom of choice for fillings. With a little practice and the right tools, pasta can be made at home quite easily.

Making Pasta

Making pasta at home may seem a daunting prospect, even for an experienced home cook.

In reality, it is quite simple provided you have the proper ingredients, tools and enough time to avoid rushing the process. Pasta dough only contains a few ingredients and, as such, you should aim to purchase the best quality you can afford when it comes to flour, eggs and olive oil. Pasta dough is often made using a special kind of flour known as '00' (double zero). This particular flour is very fine in texture and produces smooth, authentic results. Some recipes call for adding semolina flour to add additional texture and taste, however, this isn't necessary for great results. It is imperative that you have a good-quality pasta maker for rolling out your dough. Familiarise yourself with how it works before attempting to make pasta; time can be of the essence when rolling out the dough.

To serve four people you will need:

300 g / 10 ½ oz / 2 cups of '00' flour
a little extra flour, for dusting
3 medium free-range eggs
2 medium free-range yolks
2 tbsp of good quality extra-virgin olive oil (preferably Italian)
a good pinch of salt

Sift the flour onto a flat, clean work surface and make a well in the middle. Crack the eggs into the well and add the egg yolks along with a good pinch of salt. Using a fork, start to bring the flour and eggs together, drawing flour in from the outside using circular motions. Once the dough starts to roughly take shape, add the olive oil and start to knead the dough on a lightly floured surface to prevent sticking. Knead for 8–10 minutes until shiny and smooth before wrapping in cling film and chilling for at least 30 minutes.

Remove the pasta dough from the fridge and divide in half before rolling into a rectangular shape using a rolling pin; it should be thin enough to pass through the thickest setting of a pasta maker. Pass the pasta through the machine to thin it, folding it in half over itself to control the size, if necessary. Decrease the thickness setting with each pass-through of the dough until you have reached the thinnest setting on the machine. At this point you hang the pasta to dry it out. From here you can change the setting on the maker to cut the pasta sheets into shapes, such as Spaghetti. For shaped pastas, such as Penne or Garganelli, you will need a special tool called a stripper; the pasta is cut into squares or rounds and rolled against the grooves of the stripper around a small rolling pin, or pencil to create the shapes.

Making Ravioli

Once you have made your pasta dough, producing ravioli is just a step away. In addition to a pasta maker, you will need a ravioli mould tray. Follow the step for making your pasta dough all the way through to rolling the pasta out into sheets. At this point, drape a sheet of pasta over a mould before spooning your filling of choice into the moulds on top of the pasta. Place another sheet of pasta on top before sealing and cutting the ravioli by passing a rolling pin firmly over the second sheet of pasta. The ravioli should pop out of the mould when inverted. Let them dry a little on a lightly floured tray before shaking off any excess flour and cooking.

An alternative to a ravioli mould tray is a ravioli cutter, or stamper. Lay a sheet of pasta on a flat work surface and dot teaspoons of the filling in a line along the pasta, spaced apart. Run a finger dipped in water around the fillings before draping another sheet of pasta on top of the fillings, directly on top of the base sheet. Use the ravioli cutter to seal the sheets of pasta together with the filling between them. Let them dry out on a lightly floured tray before shaking off any excess flour and cooking.

Cooking Pasta

When cooking pasta, it is vitally important that you use the largest saucepan you have available. Additionally, you should add a generous amount of salt to the water before cooking; the water should taste like mild seawater and it should be at a rolling boil. For dried pastas purchased from a supermarket, follow the packet instructions for best results. Generally speaking, most kinds of dried pasta will need at least 7–8 minutes to reach 'al dente' with some sturdier styles needing 10–12 minutes. 'Al dente' is the point when the pasta is soft enough to chew whilst still retaining a little bite. Just before draining the pasta, you should scoop a cupful of the cooking liquid; this liquid is starchy and can be added to a sauce, little by little, when you are tossing the pasta to help it retain a silky texture.

When cooking fresh pasta, follow the same process, as when cooking dried, shop-bought pasta. You will, however, need to alter the cooking times because fresh pasta cooks very quickly. Sometimes it can be as quick as 1 minute, or as slow as 3 depending on the style, but it rarely takes longer than that. Once the pasta is 'al dente' drain thoroughly before tossing with sauce and a little cooking liquid. As with all kinds of pasta, serve immediately for best results.

SERVES: **4**

PREPARATION TIME: **10 MINUTES**

COOKING TIME: **10–15 MINUTES**

INGREDIENTS

2 tbsp olive oil
1 onion, roughly chopped
2 cloves of garlic, minced
75 g / 3 oz / ½ cup cherry tomatoes
a few sprigs of thyme
400 g / 14 oz / 2 cups canned chopped
   tomatoes
a pinch of caster (superfine) sugar
a small handful of basil leaves, torn
salt and freshly ground black pepper

Tomato Sauce for Pasta

1. Heat the olive oil in a large
   saucepan set over a medium heat.

2. Sauté the onion and garlic for
   5–6 minutes, stirring occasionally,
   until they start to brown.

3. Add the cherry tomatoes and thyme
   to the saucepan and cook for a
   further 2 minutes before adding
   the chopped tomatoes and sugar.

4. Stir well and simmer over a low heat
   for 10–15 minutes, until thickened.

5. Adjust the seasoning to taste
   before stirring through the basil.

6. Serve with pasta or as a
   base sauce for pizzas.

SERVES: **4**

PREPARATION TIME: **10 MINUTES**

COOKING TIME: **8–10 MINUTES**

INGREDIENTS

1 tbsp unsalted butter
1 tbsp olive oil
100 g / 3 ½ oz / ⅔ cup bacon lardons
300 g / 10 ½ oz / 3 cups dried spaghetti
100 g / 3 ½ oz / 1 cup Parmesan, finely
  grated
3 large eggs
a small handful of basil leaves
salt and freshly ground black pepper

Spaghetti a la Carbonara

1. Melt the butter and oil in a large frying pan set over a moderate heat; add the lardons and sauté for 2–3 minutes.

2. Meanwhile, cook the spaghetti in a large saucepan of boiling salted water according to packet instructions until 'al dente'; usually 8–10 minutes.

3. As the spaghetti is cooking, reduce the heat of the frying pan.

4. Whisk the eggs with seasoning and most of the Parmesan, keeping a little as a garnish.

5. Drain the spaghetti, reserving a cup of cooking water, before adding to the lardons.

6. Add the cheese and egg mixture and toss everything together, lifting well and stirring to coat evenly; adjust the seasoning to taste.

7. If the sauce is a little dry, add a little more cooking water to loosen.

8. Twist and lift the spaghetti onto plates using a meat fork, or tongs.

9. Garnish with basil leaves and Parmesan on top before serving immediately.

SERVES: **4–6**

PREPARATION TIME: **30 MINUTES**

COOKING TIME: **1 HOUR**

INGREDIENTS

2 tbsp olive oil
1 tbsp unsalted butter
1 bay leaf
1 onion, finely chopped
1 large carrot, peeled and finely chopped
1 stick of celery, peeled and chopped
2 cloves of garlic
500 g / 1 lb 2 oz / 3 ⅓ cups beef mince
400 g / 14 oz / 2 cups canned chopped
   tomatoes
150 ml / 5 fl. oz / ⅔ cup red wine
250 ml / 9 fl. oz / 1 cup beef stock
55 g / 2 oz / ½ cup Parmesan, finely
   grated
400 g / 14 oz / 4 cups dried spaghetti
a few sprigs of basil leaves, to garnish
salt and freshly ground black pepper

Spaghetti a la Bolognaise

1. Heat together the oil and butter in a large casserole dish set over a medium heat.

2. Add the bay leaf, onion, carrot and celery and sweat for 10–12 minutes until soft and golden.

3. Add the garlic and cook for 2 minutes before increasing the heat and adding the mince; brown well all over.

4. Once browned, cover with the chopped tomatoes, red wine and stock.

5. Bring to a simmer before reducing the heat to low and leaving to cook for 1 hour.

6. Stir through the Parmesan and adjust the seasoning to taste.

7. Cook the spaghetti in a large saucepan of salted, boiling water until 'al dente'; usually 8–10 minutes.

8. Drain and divide between plates before topping with the bolognaise sauce.

9. Garnish with basil before serving.

SERVES: **4**

PREPARATION TIME: **10 MINUTES**

COOKING TIME: **8–10 MINUTES**

INGREDIENTS

350 g / 12 oz / 3 ½ cups dried spaghetti
2 tbsp olive oil
1 red chilli (chili), deseeded and finely
    chopped
1 clove of garlic, minced
350 g / 12 oz / 2 ⅓ cups clams, rinsed
150 ml / 5 fl. oz / ⅔ cup dry white wine
a small bunch of flat-leaf parsley, finely
    chopped
salt and freshly ground black pepper

Linguine a la Vongole

1. Cook the spaghetti in a large saucepan of salted, boiling water until 'al dente;' usually 8–10 minutes.

2. Meanwhile, heat the olive oil in a large sauté pan set over a moderate heat.

3. Saute the chilli and garlic for 30 seconds before adding the clams and wine.

4. Cover with a lid and let the steam open the clams.

5. Once open, remove the clams from the pan; reduce the heat under the pan to low.

6. Pick the meat from the clams and set to one side.

7. Drain the spaghetti and add immediately to the pan along with the clams and parsley.

8. Toss well and adjust the seasoning to taste before serving.

SERVES: **4**

PREPARATION TIME: **10 MINUTES**

COOKING TIME: **10–12 MINUTES**

INGREDIENTS

300 g / 10 ½ oz / 3 cups dried penne
2 tbsp olive oil
1 stick of celery, sliced
1 clove of garlic, minced
450 g / 1 lb / 3 cups mussels, cleaned
   with beards removed
150 ml / 5 fl. oz / ⅔ cup dry white wine
150 g / 5 oz / 1 cup pitted black olives,
   roughly chopped
55 g / 2 oz / ½ cup Parmesan, grated
a small handful of basil leaves
1 lemon, cut into wedges
salt and freshly ground black pepper

Penne with Mussels

1. Cook the penne in a large saucepan of salted, boiling water until 'al dente'; 10–12 minutes usually.

2. Meanwhile, heat the olive oil in a large sauté pan set over a moderate heat.

3. Sauté the celery and garlic for 1 minute before adding the mussels and wine.

4. Cover with a lid and let the steam cook the mussels until they open; remove the mussels

from the pan and pick out the meat from the shells.

5. Drain the penne when ready and add to the pan along with the mussel meat and olives.

6. Toss well to coat before spooning into bowls.

7. Garnish with Parmesan, basil leaves and lemon wedges before serving.

SERVES: **4**

PREPARATION TIME: **15–20 MINUTES**

COOKING TIME: **8–10 MINUTES**

INGREDIENTS

300 g / 10 ½ oz / 3 cups rigatoni
250 g / 9 oz / 2 cups soft goats' cheese
2 tbsp olive oil
1 clove of garlic, minced
1 small aubergine, deseeded and finely diced
a small bunch of mint leaves, finely chopped
salt and freshly ground black pepper

Goats' Cheese Rigatoni

1. Cook the rigatoni in a saucepan of salted, boiling water until 'al dente'; 8–10 minutes usually.

2. Drain and leave to cool before patting dry.

3. Stuff the rigatoni with the soft goats' cheese and set to one side.

4. Heat the olive oil in a large sauté pan set over a medium heat.

5. Add the garlic and aubergine and sauté for 4–5 minutes, stirring occasionally, until golden.

6. Add the stuffed rigatoni and mint, stir once, and continue to cook untouched for 2 minutes.

7. Adjust the seasoning to taste before serving.

SERVES: **6–8**

PREPARATION TIME: **I HR 30 MINUTES**

COOKING TIME: **2 HOURS**

INGREDIENTS

2 tbsp olive oil
I onion, finely chopped
I large carrot, peeled and finely chopped
I stick of celery, peeled and chopped
2 cloves of garlic
500 g / I lb 2 oz / 3 ⅓ cups beef mince
400 g / 14 oz / 2 cups canned chopped
   tomatoes
150 ml / 5 fl. oz / ⅔ cup red wine
250 ml / 9 fl. oz / I cup beef stock
2 tbsp unsalted butter, plus extra
   for greasing
2 tbsp plain (all purpose) flour
500 ml / I lb 2 oz / 2 cups whole milk
a pinch of ground nutmeg
400 g / 14 oz / 4 cups dried lasagne sheets
100 g / 3 ½ oz / I cup Cheddar, grated
I bay leaf
salt and freshly ground black pepper

Lasagne

1. Heat the oil in a large casserole dish set over a medium heat; sweat the chopped vegetables for 10–12 minutes.

2. Add the garlic and cook for 2 minutes; increase the heat and add the mince, browning well all over.

3. Once browned, cover with the chopped tomatoes, red wine and stock.

4. Bring to a simmer before reducing the heat to low and leaving to cook for I hour; adjust the seasoning to taste and set to one side.

5. Melt the butter in a saucepan set over a moderate heat before whisking in the flour to make a roux; cook until golden.

6. Whisk in the milk in a slow, steady stream until a sauce forms; simmer for 5 minutes before adding the nutmeg and seasoning.

7. Preheat the oven to 180°C (160°C fan) / 350F / gas 4 and grease a large rectangular baking dish with a little butter.

8. Spread a little white sauce over the base before topping a layer of lasagne sheets.

9. Top with meat sauce, more white sauce and then a layer of lasagne sheets.

10. Repeat the process again, finishing with a layer of white sauce.

11. Sprinkle over the grated Cheddar and place the bay leaf in the centre; bake for I hour until golden on top and piping hot throughout before serving.

SERVES: **6**

PREPARATION TIME: **20 MINUTES**

COOKING TIME: **25–30 MINUTES**

INGREDIENTS

450 g / 1 lb / 4 cups dried macaroni
2 tbsp unsalted butter, plus extra for greasing
2 tbsp plain (all purpose) flour
500 ml / 18 fl. oz / 2 cups whole milk
1 large egg yolk
a small bunch of basil leaves, chopped
100 g / 3 ½ oz / 1 cup Cheddar, grated
salt and freshly ground black pepper

Macaroni Gratin

1. Preheat the oven to 190°C (170°C fan) / 375F / gas 5.

2. Cook the macaroni in a large saucepan of salted, boiling water for 8 minutes; drain and leave to dry to one side.

3. Melt the butter in a large saucepan set over a moderate heat before whisking in the flour to make a roux; cook until golden in appearance.

4. Whisk in the milk in a slow, steady stream until a thickened sauce forms; simmer for 5 minutes before adding the egg yolk, basil and half of the Cheddar, stirring well to incorporate.

5. Add the macaroni to the saucepan and stir well to coat in the sauce; adjust the seasoning to taste.

6. Grease a large rectangular baking dish with butter before spooning in the macaroni.

7. Sprinkle over the remaining Cheddar before baking for 25–30 minutes until golden on top.

8. Remove from the oven and leave to stand for a few minutes before serving.

RICE

Types of Rice

As one of the most commonly grown crops in the world, there are a multitude of rice varieties, all with different uses in the kitchen. Fragrant rices, such as basmati and jasmine are the ideal accompaniment to Indian and Thai curries. Short-grain styles, such as Arborio, or Calasparra are perfect for Italian risottos and Spanish paellas. Pudding rice is a short-grain variety often used to prepare rice pudding. Furthermore, there are long-grain types, such as American long-grain that can be used in rice salads, as well as wild rice varieties that are great in salads and as a healthy accompaniment to roasted meats, or fish. Each kind of rice has an optimum use, just as each kind of rice can't be used for all purposes. Matching the kind of rice to the dish will give you the best results possible.

Some rice varieties need to be washed thoroughly before using. Basmati is a prime example of this – it should be rinsed thoroughly in several changes of water to get rid of excess starch that can make the rice sticky when cooked. A variety, such as pudding rice, does not need to be rinsed before use because it can simply be cooked as sold. Rice has the advantage of being gluten-free; perfect for those who struggle with carbohydrates, such as bread or pasta. Just like pasta, it is nutritious and can be used in a plethora of dishes from stir-fries to desserts.

Cooking Rice

Before cooking your rice, you need to know whether you should rinse it or not. As highlighted above, rice such as basmati needs to be rinsed thoroughly before cooking. Other rice varieties that benefit from rinsing include long-grain American rice and wild rice varieties. The package instructions should indicate whether it is best to rinse your rice.

For boiling rice, such as basmati, fry the rice first in a little hot sunflower or vegetable oil in a large saucepan to release the fragrant aromas. Cover the volume of rice you are cooking with one inch of liquid - hot water or stock would be ideal. Bring the liquid to a simmer before lowering the heat. Once the rice has absorbed most of the liquid and is tender, remove the saucepan from the heat and drain before leaving to cool to one side, still covered. Season and use as needed.

For steaming rice, such as jasmine, repeat the process as for basmati rice above until you add the liquid. Once the liquid has been added to the rice and is simmering, cover the saucepan with a lid and reduce the heat to low. Let the rice cook until it has absorbed all the liquid. Remove the saucepan from the heat and leave to cool, still covered, for at least 5–10 minutes before fluffing with a fork and serving.

For wild rice, the ratio of rice to liquid needs to be approximately 1:3. Add the rice to a large saucepan with a little salt and cover it with three times the volume of hot liquid. Bring to the boil before reducing to a low simmer – depending on your volume of rice this could take 30–60 minutes to cook until tender. Once the kernels pop open, you will know that the rice is ready. Drain any excess liquid before leaving to steam for a few minutes. Fluff with a fork before serving.

Long-grain varieties follow similar principles to cooking basmati and jasmine; adjust the ratio of rice to liquid to 1:2. Long-grain rice can either be boiled or steamed.

INGREDIENTS

2 tbsp olive oil
1 shallot, finely chopped
2 cloves of garlic, minced
200 g / 7 oz / 1 cup Arborio rice
110 ml / 4 fl. oz / ½ cup dry white wine
1.2 l / 2 pints 4 fl. oz / 5 cups vegetable
 stock, hot
75 ml / 3 fl. oz / ⅓ cup double (heavy) cream
55 g / 2 oz / ¼ cup Parmesan, finely grated
2 tbsp unsalted butter
150 g / 5 oz / 2 cups button mushrooms,
 cleaned and halved
a small bunch of flat-leaf parsley, chopped
salt and freshly ground black pepper

Mushroom Risotto

1. Heat the olive oil in a large heavy-based saucepan over a medium heat.

2. Sauté the shallot gently for 4–5 minutes then add the garlic and continue to cook for a further 2 minutes.

3. Add the rice and coat thoroughly in the oil; cook for 3–4 minutes, or until the grains start to turn translucent.

4. Add the white wine and increase the heat to allow it to evaporate almost entirely.

5. Add the hot stock to the risotto a ladle at a time, stirring frequently, until each ladle of stock is absorbed into the rice.

6. Continue in this fashion until all the stock has been absorbed and the rice is soft, yet still defined; usually 30–40 minutes.

7. Stir through the cream and Parmesan and adjust the seasoning to taste before keeping warm to one side.

8. Melt the butter in a large sauté, or frying pan set over a moderate heat.

9. Sauté the mushrooms for 5–6 minutes, stirring occasionally, until golden and tender.

10. Stir into the risotto along with the parsley and ladle into bowls before serving.

SERVES: **4**

PREPARATION TIME: **10 MINUTES**

COOKING TIME: **25–30 MINUTES**

INGREDIENTS

1 l / 1 pint 16 fl. oz / 4 cups whole milk
75 g / 3 oz / ⅓ cup caster (superfine) sugar
1 vanilla pod, split with seeds scraped out
200 g / 7 oz / 1 cup pudding rice
2 tbsp double (heavy) cream
a pinch of nutmeg

Simple Rice Pudding

1. Combine the milk, sugar, vanilla pod and seeds in a saucepan; bring to boiling point over a moderate heat before reducing to a low heat.

2. Add the rice, stir well and fish out the vanilla pod at this point.

3. Cook over a low heat, stirring frequently, until the rice has absorbed the milk and is tender; 25–30 minutes.

4. Once the rice is tender and has absorbed most of the milk, stir through the cream and nutmeg.

5. The pudding can be served warm, or chilled.

SERVES: **4**

PREPARATION TIME: **10 MINUTES**

COOKING TIME: **10 MINUTES**

INGREDIENTS

2 tbsp sesame, or groundnut oil
1 large courgette (zucchini), sliced
2 medium carrots, peeled and cut into
   thin strips
1 small onion, sliced
200 g / 7 oz / 1 ⅓ cups firm tofu, cubed
350 g / 12 oz / 2 cups cooked
   medium-grain white rice
1 spring onion (scallion), finely sliced
150 g / 5 oz / 1 ½ cups canned
   sweetcorn, drained
2 tbsp dark soy sauce
½ tbsp rice wine vinegar
1 tbsp sesame seeds, toasted

Fried Rice with Tofu and Carrots

1. Heat the oil in a large wok set over a moderate heat until hot.

2. Add the courgette, carrots and onion and stir-fry for 2–3 minutes until tender.

3. Add the tofu to the wok and continue to stir-fry for 2–3 minutes before removing everything from the wok.

4. Reduce the heat a little and add the rice; cook for 3–4 minutes until warmed through.

5. Stir through the spring onion and sweetcorn before seasoning to taste using soy sauce and rice wine vinegar.

6. Spoon into bowls and top with the vegetables and a sprinkling of sesame seeds before serving.

SERVES: **4**

PREPARATION TIME: **15 MINUTES**

COOKING TIME: **12–15 MINUTES**

INGREDIENTS

2 tbsp sunflower oil
1 bay leaf
½ stick of cinnamon
½ tsp cumin seeds
1 clove of garlic, crushed
1 onion, sliced
200 g / 7 oz / 2 cups basmati rice,
    rinsed in several changes of cold
    water and drained
400 ml / 14 fl. oz / 2 cups vegetable
    stock, hot
a few sprigs of coriander (cilantro), to
    garnish
salt and pepper

Pilaf Rice

1. Heat the sunflower oil in a
large saucepan set over a
moderate heat until hot.

2. Add the bay leaf, cinnamon, cumin
seeds and garlic and sauté for 30
seconds before adding the onion.

3. Continue to sauté for 2–3 minutes
until the onion starts to brown.

4. Add the rice and one teaspoon
of salt; stir well to coat in the oil
before covering with the hot stock.

5. Stir once and bring the liquid to
a simmer before covering and
cooking over a reduced heat
until the rice has absorbed the
liquid: 12–15 minutes usually.

6. Remove from the heat and leave
the rice covered to one side for 10
minutes before fluffing with a fork
and adjusting the seasoning to taste.

7. Serve with a sprig of
coriander as a garnish.

SERVES: **4**

PREPARATION TIME: **15 MINUTES**

COOKING TIME: **25–30 MINUTES**

INGREDIENTS

2 tbsp sunflower oil
1 onion, finely chopped
2 sticks of celery, finely chopped
1 red pepper, deseeded and finely chopped
1 tbsp tomato purée
225 g / 8 oz / 1 ½ cups Andouille sausage, or
     chorizo, peeled and sliced
2 tsp Cajun seasoning
300 g / 10 ½ oz / 3 cups long-grain white
     rice, rinsed in several changes of cold
     water and drained
450 g / 1 lb / 3 cups prawns (shrimp),
     deveined
450 ml / 16 fl. oz / 2 cups chicken stock, hot
a few sprigs of thyme, to garnish
salt and freshly ground black pepper

Jambalaya

1. Heat the oil in a large
    saucepan, or casserole dish
    set over a medium heat.

2. Sweat the onion, celery and
    pepper for 5–6 minutes
    until softened before stirring
    through the tomato purée.

3. Cook for 1 minute before adding
    the sausage, or chorizo.

4. Continue to cook for 2
    minutes before adding the
    Cajun seasoning and rice.

5. Stir well before adding the prawns
    and stock; stir again thoroughly.

6. Bring the liquid to a simmer before
    covering with a lid and cooking
    over a gentle, low heat for 25–30
    minutes until the rice is tender.

7. Adjust the seasoning to taste
    before spooning into bowls
    and garnishing with thyme.

SERVES: **4**

PREPARATION TIME: **15 MINUTES**

COOKING TIME: **25 MINUTES**

INGREDIENTS

2 medium eggs
I tbsp sunflower oil
I onion, finely chopped
I bay leaf
110 g / 4 oz / I cup basmati rice, rinsed
   in several changes of cold water and
   drained
225 ml / 8 fl. oz / I cup hot water
300 g / 10 ½ oz / 2 cups un-dyed
   smoked haddock
500 ml / 18 fl. oz / 2 cups whole milk
I tbsp unsalted butter
I tbsp plain (all purpose) flour
I tbsp Madras curry powder
a pinch of ground nutmeg
a few chive stalks, finely chopped
wholemeal bread, to serve
salt and freshly ground black pepper

Haddock Kedgeree

1. Cook the eggs in a large saucepan of boiling water for 10 minutes; drain and refresh in iced water.

2. Heat the oil in a large saucepan set over a moderate heat; sauté the onion and bay leaf for 3–4 minutes.

3. Stir in the drained rice and cook for I minute before covering with the hot water and simmer.

4. Cover with a lid and cook over a reduced heat until the rice has absorbed the liquid; 12–15 minutes.

5. Meanwhile, place the haddock and milk in a saucepan, boil then simmer and poach for 4–5 minutes until the fish is firm with a little spring to the touch.

6. Remove the haddock and leave to cool to one side; pour the milk into a jug.

7. Melt the butter in the saucepan before whisking in the flour to make a roux; cook until golden before whisking in the curry powder and nutmeg.

8. Whisk in the milk in a slow-steady stream until thickened; simmer for 5 minutes over a low heat before seasoning.

9. Fluff the cooked rice with a fork and stir half into the curry sauce; flake the haddock and add to the rice.

10. Peel the eggs and finely chop before spooning the kedgeree into serving pots.

11. Spoon the remaining rice over and garnish with chopped egg and chives; serve with bread.

PASTRY

Types of Pastry

There are three main kinds of pastry, shortcrust (sweet and savoury), puff and choux. There are additional variations, such as hot water pastry, but these fall within the broader categories of the main three.

Shortcrust is probably the most commonly used pastry. It is easily adapted for sweet and savoury uses and is versatile enough to be used in several applications. Savoury shortcrust pastry has only four ingredients; flour, butter, salt and water. It can be enriched with the addition of egg, but this isn't necessary for good results. Sweet shortcrust pastry is ideal for use in pies and patisserie desserts. It is often enriched with egg, or egg yolks, taking the place of water to bind the pastry. Both kinds of pastry are fairly robust and can be shaped into a variety of different moulds and tins.

Making puff pastry takes practice and more than one go to master. Once you have learned the practical basics of making puff pastry, it is just a matter of time and patience. Whereas shortcrust pastry can be brought together relatively quickly, the same cannot be said for puff pastry. It takes a little more time and effort, but is definitely worth the outlay, especially for special recipes, such as Beef Wellington, or patisserie treats.

Choux pastry is often called for when making delicate canapés or classical French desserts, such as profiteroles. It is prepared differently to shortcrust and puff pastry and is typically enriched with a high proportion of eggs and butter for richness and taste.

Shortcrust Pastry

Learning how to make shortcrust pastry opens up the door to several dishes, both sweet and savoury. The best shortcrust pastry is made with a lightness of touch for a crumbly texture. Shortcrust pastry needs to be rested before using in order to give the processed gluten time to relax and prevent the pastry from shrinking too much. You can make it by hand, or by using a food processor, which can reduce the time taken.

To make 350 g / 12 oz of shortcrust pastry, you will need:

250 g / 9 oz / 1 ⅔ cups plain flour
a pinch of salt
110 g / 4 oz / ½ cup unsalted butter, cold and cubed
50–75 ml / 2–3 fl. oz / ¼–⅓ cup iced water

Sift together the flour and salt into a mixing bowl, or a food processor, if using. Rub the cubes of cold butter into the flour in a mixing bowl, until it resembles breadcrumbs. If using a food processor, pulse the mixture briefly until it resembles breadcrumbs. Add a little of the water and mix into the dough, gently, until a rough dough starts to form. In a food processor, pulse briefly until a ball of dough starts to come together. Add a little more water if the dough appears too dry. If it appears too wet, add a little more flour. Turn the dough out onto a lightly floured surface and gently knead for 1 minute before shaping into a ball. Wrap in cling film and chill for at least 30 minutes before rolling out and using.

When making sweet shortcrust pastry, add 1 tbsp of caster sugar to the flour and repeat the process as above.

Simple Puff Pastry

Simple puff pastry is great for using in savoury and sweet tarts. You can top it with vegetables and goats' cheese for a quick dinner or top with strawberries and a little jam for a quick dessert.

To make 350 g / 12 oz of simple puff pastry, you will need:

125 g / 4 ½ oz / ¾ cup strong plain white flour
a pinch of salt
125 g / 4 ½ oz / ½ cup unsalted butter, at room temperature
125–150 ml / 4 ½–5 fl. oz / ⅓–½ cup iced water

Sift the flour and salt into a mixing bowl. Break the butter into small chunks and add them to the bowl, rubbing them in loosely. Rather than rubbing them in until the mixture resembles breadcrumbs, you need to be able to see chunks of the butter amongst the flour. Make a well in the middle of the mixture and add approximately two-thirds of the water, mixing until a dough starts to form. Add a little more water if the dough is too dry. Cover and chill for at least 20 minutes.

Turn out the dough onto a lightly floured surface and knead briefly before shaping into a rectangle. Roll the rectangle out until it reaches approximately 15 cm x 40 cm (6 in x 16 in) in dimension; the dough should appear marbled from the butter. Fold the top down over the middle before folding the bottom up and over the top fold. Turn the dough 90° to the right before rolling out to the same dimensions as before. Fold again in the same fashion before covering and chilling for at least 30 minutes. You can now use the dough after chilling.

Choux Pastry

Choux pastry is very much a two-step process; the dough is prepared in a saucepan before being spooned into a piping bag and piped onto a tray. It is then baked in a hot oven before being filled and served.

To make approximately 450 g / 1 lb of savoury choux pastry, you will need:

a pinch of salt
250 ml / 9 fl. oz / 1 cup cold water
100 g / 3 ½ oz / ½ cup unsalted butter, cold and cubed
110 g / 4 oz / ⅔ cup plain flour, sifted
4 medium eggs, beaten

Start by preheating your oven to 200°C (180°C fan) / 400F / gas 6; line a large baking tray with greaseproof paper. Combine the salt, water and butter in a saucepan and heat over a medium heat until the butter has melted. Once the mixture comes to the boil, remove the pan from the heat and add the flour. Beat vigorously until the mixture starts to pull away from the sides of the pan. Beat in the eggs, a little at time, until fully incorporated and the dough is glossy and thick. Spoon into a piping bag fitted with a nozzle. Pipe blobs of the dough onto the baking tray, spaced apart, before baking for 15–20 minutes until golden brown and risen. Remove to a wire rack to cool before serving or filling.

For sweet choux pastry, it is advisable to replace the water with milk and add 1 tbsp of sugar to the flour.

Tarts and Flans

Most tarts and flans work best when using shortcrust pastry. Quiches, for example, work best with savoury shortcrust as do fruit flans. A fruit tart would be ideally made with puff pastry.

For a savoury tart, prepare a batch of savoury shortcrust pastry. Roll the pastry out on a lightly floured surface to ½ cm (¼ in) thickness before draping it over an 20 cm (8 in) tart tin. Press the pastry into the base and sides of the tin before cutting away any overhanging excess pastry with a sharp knife. Re-roll the excess pastry into a ball and chill for another use. Prick the base of the lined pastry with a fork before lining the tin with greaseproof paper and baking beans. Bake the pastry in an oven preheated to 190°C (170°C fan) / 375F / gas 5 (known as blind-baking) for 12–15 minutes until the corners are golden. Remove the pastry from the oven and discard the baking beans and greaseproof paper. The base can now be brushed with beaten egg and the pastry returned to the oven for a few minutes to glaze. Remove the pastry and fill with beaten egg and cream, for example, for a quiche before returning to a reduced oven to finish cooking.

SERVES: **4–6**

PREPARATION TIME: **15–20 MINUTES**

COOKING TIME: **45–55 MINUTES**

INGREDIENTS

250 g / 9 oz ready-made shortcrust pastry
a little plain (all purpose) flour, for dusting
175 ml / 6 fl. oz / ¾ cup whole milk
225 g / 8 oz / 1 cup crème fraiche
4 large eggs
2 tbsp Dijon mustard
100 g / 3 ½ oz / 1 cup Gruyere, finely grated
a large bunch of chive stalks
salt and freshly ground black pepper

Chive and Mustard Quiche

1. Preheat the oven to 160°C (140°C fan) / 325F / gas 3.

2. Roll out the pastry on a floured surface to ½ cm (¼ in) thickness and use to line a 18 cm (7 in) tart tin; prick the base with a fork and chill.

3. Whisk together the milk, crème fraiche, eggs, mustard and seasoning until smooth.

4. Finely chop most of the chive stalks before whisking into the milk and egg mixture along with half of the Gruyere.

5. Pour the filling into the chilled pastry case and top with the remaining Gruyere.

6. Bake for 45–55 minutes until the pastry is golden and cooked and the filling is set with a very slight wobble at the middle.

7. Remove from the oven and leave to cool before turning out and serving with extra chives on top.

SERVES: **4–6**

PREPARATION TIME: **15–20 MINUTES**

COOKING TIME: **45–50 MINUTES**

INGREDIENTS

200 g / 7 oz ready-made shortcrust pastry
a little plain (all purpose) flour, for dusting
2 large eggs
75 g / 3 oz / ⅓ cup caster (superfine) sugar
100 g / 3 ½ oz / ⅔ cup self-raising flour
150 ml / 5 fl. oz / ⅔ cup whole milk
½ tsp vanilla extract
2 tbsp unsalted butter, melted
450 g / 1 lb / 3 cups ripe figs, halved
a few sprigs of thyme, to garnish

Fig Pie

1. Preheat the oven to 160°C (140°C fan) / 325F / gas 3.

2. Roll out the pastry on a lightly floured surface to ½ cm (¼ in) thickness; use it to line a 18 cm (7 in) pie dish, pressing well into the sides and bases; trim any excess overhanging pastry.

3. Beat together the eggs and sugar in a mixing bowl until smooth before folding through the flour.

4. Whisk in the milk, vanilla extract and melted butter in that order, until you have a smooth batter.

5. Pour into the pastry case and arrange the fig halves in it.

6. Bake for 45–50 minutes until the pastry is golden and the batter is set; remove from the oven and garnish with thyme on top before serving.

SERVES: **4–6**

PREPARATION TIME: **2–2 ¼ HOURS**

COOKING TIME: **25–30 MINUTES**

INGREDIENTS

2 tbsp sunflower oil
750 g / 1 lb 10 oz / 5 cups stewing steak, trimmed and evenly diced
1 onion, chopped
150 g / 5 oz / 1 cup lamb's kidneys, cored and diced
2 tbsp plain (all purpose) flour, plus extra for dusting
850 ml / 1 pint 10 fl. oz / 3 ½ cups beef stock
a dash of Worcestershire sauce
a small bunch of flat-leaf parsley, finely chopped
200 g / 7 oz ready-made puff pastry
1 small egg, beaten
salt and freshly ground black pepper

Steak and Kidney Pie

1. Heat the oil in a large casserole dish set over a moderate heat, until hot.

2. Season the steak and seal in batches, until golden all over, before removing from the dish and draining on kitchen paper.

3. Reduce the heat under the dish and sauté the onion in the accumulated oil until golden; 3–4 minutes.

4. Return the steak to the dish along with the kidneys and flour; stir well and cook for 1 minute before covering with the stock and Worcestershire sauce.

5. Bring to a simmer and cook steadily for 1 ½–1 ¾ hours, uncovered, until the steak is tender.

6. Adjust the seasoning to taste and stir through the parsley before spooning into a square baking dish; preheat the oven to 220°C (200°C fan) / 425F / gas 7.

7. Roll out the pastry on a lightly floured surface into a square with ½ cm (¼ in) thickness; drape over the baking dish, sealing against the edges before cutting away any excess pastry.

8. Brush the top with the beaten egg and bore a small hole in the middle before baking for 25–30 minutes, until the pastry is golden and risen.

SERVES: **6**

PREPARATION TIME: **20–25 MINUTES**

COOKING TIME: **35–45 MINUTES**

INGREDIENTS

4 sheets of ready-made filo pastry, kept under
  a damp towel
2 tbsp olive oil
1 onion, finely chopped
1 red onion, finely chopped
½ tsp dried oregano
½ tsp dried thyme
300 g / 10 ½ oz / 6 cups baby spinach, washed
400 g / 14 oz / 2 ½ cups ricotta
200 g / 7 oz / 2 cups feta, crumbled
2 tbsp unsalted butter, melted
salt and freshly ground black pepper

Spanakopita

1. Preheat the oven to 200°C (180°C fan) / 400F / gas 6; line a 18 cm (7 in) springform cake tin with a sheet of greaseproof paper on its base and sides.

2. Heat the oil in a large saucepan set over a moderate heat until hot; sauté the onions in the oil for 6–7 minutes, stirring frequently, until golden at the edges.

3. Add the dried herbs, stir well, and add the spinach; let it cook down and wilt over a reduced heat before removing from the heat.

4. Drain the spinach and onions through a colander before roughly chopping and placing in a mixing bowl.

5. Add the ricotta and feta and mix well with your hands; adjust the seasoning to taste.

6. Line the prepared tin with a couple of sheets of filo pastry, before spooning the filling on top, smoothing with the back of a tablespoon.

7. Drape the remaining filo sheets on top, tucking the edges over and in before brushing the top with melted butter.

8. Bake for 35–45 minutes until golden on top; remove from the oven and leave to cool a little before turning out and serving.

INGREDIENTS

55 g / 2 oz / ¼ cup unsalted butter
1.25 kg / 3 lb / 10 ⅔ cups Granny Smith
   apples, peeled, cored and sliced
110 g / 4 oz / ½ cup caster (superfine) sugar
100 g / 3 ½ oz / ⅔ cup raisins
1 lemon, juiced
300 g / 10 ½ oz ready-made wholewheat
   shortcrust pastry
a little plain (all purpose) flour, for dusting
2 tbsp icing (confectioners') sugar, for
   dusting

Apple and Raisin Pie

1. Preheat the oven to 180°C
   (160°C fan) / 350F / gas 4 and line
   a 20 cm (8 in) springform cake
   tin with greaseproof paper.

2. Melt the butter in a heavy-based
   saucepan and cook the apples with
   the raisins, sugar and lemon juice for
   5–7 minutes, stirring occasionally,
   until slightly softened; set to one side.

3. Roll out the pastry on a lightly
   floured surface, cut out a 25 cm
   (10 in) round, approximately
   1 cm (½ in) thick and line the tin with

it before gathering up the remaining
pastry and re-rolling into an 20cm
(8 in) round that is 1 cm (½ in) thick.

4. Fill the lined pastry with the apple
   filling and place the other round
   on top, sealing well, before making
   slits on top with a sharp knife.

5. Bake for 40–45 minutes before
   removing to a wire rack to cool;
   turn out carefully and dust with
   icing sugar before serving

MAKES: **24**

PREPARATION TIME: **15–20 MINUTES**

COOKING TIME: **10–12 MINUTES**

INGREDIENTS

350 g / 12 oz ready-made puff pastry
a little plain flour, for dusting
55 g / 2 oz / ¼ cup unsalted butter, melted
150 g / 5 oz / 1 ½ cups Cheddar, finely grated
salt and freshly ground black pepper

Cheese Flaky Pastry Twists

1. Preheat the oven to 220°C (200°C fan) / 425F / gas 7 and line a baking tray with greaseproof paper.

2. Roll out the pastry on a lightly floured surface into a square with ½ cm (¼ in) thickness; trim the edges and discard.

3. Cut the square in half before brushing with melted butter and sprinkling over the grated Cheddar onto both pieces.

4. Cut each piece into straw shapes, approximately 1 cm (½ in) wide, and arrange on the baking tray; pinch the ends and twist the straws in opposite directions to shape them into braids. Season with a little salt and pepper.

5. Bake for 10–12 minutes until risen and golden before removing to a wire rack to cool before serving.

SERVES: 6

PREPARATION TIME: 30–35 MINUTES

COOKING TIME: 20–30 MINUTES

INGREDIENTS

2 tbsp sunflower oil
750 g / 1 lb 10 oz piece of beef fillet,
    trimmed
2 tbsp unsalted butter
450 g / 1 lb / 6 cups button mushrooms,
    finely chopped
a small bunch of flat-leaf parsley, finely
    chopped
½ lemon, juiced
250 g / 9 oz ready-made puff pastry
a little plain (all purpose) flour, for dusting
8–10 slices of prosciutto
1 large egg, beaten
salt and freshly ground black pepper

Beef Wellington

1. Preheat the oven to 200°C (180°C fan) / 400F / gas 6.

2. Coat the beef in the oil and season generously; heat a large frying, or sauté pan over a moderate heat until hot.

3. Seal the beef until golden all over; remove from the pan and leave to rest to one side.

4. Melt the butter in the frying pan over a reduced heat before adding the chopped mushrooms; sauté for 8–10 minutes, stirring frequently.

5. Stir through the parsley and adjust the seasoning to taste using lemon juice, salt and pepper.

6. Spoon the mushrooms onto a tray lined with kitchen paper to drain.

7. Roll out the pastry into a rectangle approximately 30 cm x 20 cm (12 in x 8 in) with ½ cm (¼ in) thickness; lift onto a large baking tray.

8. Lay the slices of prosciutto on top, overlapping to cover the pastry; spoon a layer of mushroom duxelle on top and sit the beef fillet on top before spooning over

the remaining mushrooms.

9. Lift the pastry up and around the top of the mushrooms; seal well on top and at the ends to envelop the filling.

10. Brush all over with the beaten egg and score lightly on top with a knife to make a pattern.

11. Bake for 20–30 minutes until the pastry is golden and the beef is cooked in the middle to your liking.

12. Remove from the oven and leave to rest for a few minutes before slicing and serving.

SERVES: **4**

PREPARATION TIME: **25–30 MINUTES**

COOKING TIME: **20–25 MINUTES**

INGREDIENTS

150 g / 5 oz / 1 cup plain (all purpose) flour
a pinch of salt
2 tsp caster (superfine) sugar
125 ml / 4 ½ fl. oz / ½ cup water
125 ml / 4 ½ fl. oz / ½ cup whole milk
110 g / 4 oz / ½ cup unsalted butter, diced
5 medium eggs
375 ml / 13 fl. oz / 1 ½ cups double (heavy)
　　cream
100 g / 3 ½ oz / ⅔ cup dark chocolate,
　　chopped
1 tbsp golden syrup
125 g / 4 ½ oz / 1 cup icing (confectioners')
　　sugar
2–3 tbsp boiling water
2 tbsp white chocolate sprinkles

Profiteroles with Chocolate Sauce

1. Preheat the oven to 200°C (180°C fan) / 400F / gas 6 and line a large baking tray with greaseproof paper.

2. Sift together the flour, salt and sugar into a mixing bowl.

3. Combine the water, milk and butter in a saucepan and bring to a simmer, stirring, until the butter has melted.

4. Bring the liquid to the boil and beat in the flour mixture, removing from the heat temporarily, before returning over a reduced heat.

5. Beat until you have a smooth dough; beat in the eggs, one at a time, off heat until shiny.

6. Spoon into a piping bag fitted with a straight-sided nozzle and pipe blobs onto the tray.

7. Bake for 10 minutes before reducing the heat to 160°C (140°C fan) / 325F / gas 3 and baking for a further 10–15 minutes until golden-brown and crisp; remove to a wire rack to cool.

8. Once cool, whip the cream in a mixing bowl until stiffly peaked; spoon into a piping bag fitted with a straight-sided nozzle.

9. Bore small holes in the base of the buns and pipe in the cream to fill.

10. Melt the chocolate and golden syrup in a heatproof bowl set atop a saucepan of simmering water, until smooth; remove to one side to cool and thicken.

11. Whisk together the icing sugar with enough boiling water to make a pourable icing; dip the tops of the buns in the icing and arrange in bowls.

12. Garnish with white chocolate sprinkles and chocolate sauce on top before serving.

BREAD

Types of Bread

Bread is a universal staple with almost every country's cuisine having a version to call its own. From leavened to unleavened styles, bread has been a popular and daily essential for most people throughout history. Without bread, there would be no sandwiches for lunch, or toast in the morning at breakfast.

When it comes to leavened bread, there are styles aplenty from rye to sourdough to baguettes. Bagels are regularly served at breakfast and brunch, not to forget the humble sandwich loaf when it comes to lunchtime. Brioche is an example of a style of leavened bread that uses butter and eggs to enrich the dough. Similar to brioche is challah bread; a Jewish specialty often prepared for the Sabbath. Italian cuisine gives us focaccia and ciabatta breads, both examples of leavened breads. All these breads make use of a leavening agent, whether that's yeast, buttermilk or a sourdough starter, to promote the release of gas to give the bread its rise.

Unleavened breads tend to be easier to prepare, but are no less delicious. Flatbreads are probably the most recognisable style of unleavened bread in cuisine around the world. In Mexican cuisine, flour tortillas play a role in dishes, such as burritos, fajitas and enchiladas. Rotis and chapattis are prime examples of unleavened breads in Indian cuisine, where the storage and cost of leavening agents tends to prohibit the production of leavened styles of bread in that part of the world.

Making Leavened Bread

Making leavened bread requires a leavening agent in order to produce the steam that will make the dough rise. A classic example of a leavening agent is baker's yeast, which can be found in active and dried varieties. Fast action dried yeast is a quick and effective way of replicating active yeast, which can be hard to source for home cooks. If you are able to source fresh yeast, you will need to convert the dried yeast to fresh yeast amount in the ratio of 1:1 ½ i.e. if the recipe calls for 20 g of dried yeast, use 30 g of fresh yeast. One of the most important ingredients in bread making is flour; it is the main ingredient around which bread is made. When selecting a type of flour, supermarkets sell versions called strong bread flour, which have a higher protein content and gluten strength to promote rising.

Another key component in making leavened bread is the liquid, which is usually tepid water. It's important that the liquid is introduced to the yeast at the optimum temperature to promote activation of the yeast, which happens around 30°C. A quick way to reach a tepid temperature is to mix two parts cold water with one part boiling. Bear in mind that if the liquid is too hot, or cold, the yeast will not activate properly. Finally, sugar is often added to provide 'food' for the yeast to activate.

Having assembled the ingredients to prepare your dough, the yeast, sugar and water is briefly mixed in a jug with a little salt. It is then left to activate in a warm space for approximately 15 minutes until frothy. The yeast mixture is added to the flour and mixed well until a ball of dough comes together. It is then turned out onto a floured surface to be kneaded for 5–7 minutes until smooth and elastic. Then comes the first proving stage; the dough is placed in a clean bowl and covered loosely before leaving to prove in a warm space until doubled in size. After doubling in size, it can now be punched down and shaped into either a loaf tin, or divided into rolls. You can also add extra ingredients at this point, such as herbs and dried fruit. It is given another 30 minutes to prove for a second time before being baked in a moderate oven, until golden and risen. You can tell when the bread is ready, as it will sound hollow when tapped on its base.

Making Unleavened Bread

As outlined previously, making unleavened bread is a little simpler and less time consuming than making leavened. You can make a batch of dough in less than 30 minutes by simply mixing together flour, warm water and salt. Some recipes benefit from the addition of a little oil, or butter to the dough. For a simple flatbread, try mixing flour with half the amount of liquid and a few tablespoons of olive oil. Add a generous pinch of salt, or seasonings and mix until a rough dough comes together. Knead the dough for 4–5 minutes until smooth and elastic before leaving to rest for 15 minutes. Divide the dough into small balls before rolling out on a lightly floured surface to approximately 1 cm (½ in) thickness. Cook on a hot griddle pan or flat frying pan for 2 minutes on each side until golden. Serve straight away with accompaniments of your choice.

Simple Bread

Here is a quick 'how to' for making a simple loaf of bread. To make one large loaf you will need:

600 ml / 1 pint 2 fl. oz / 3 cups tepid water
2 tbsp dried fast-action yeast (or 3 tbsp fresh yeast)
2 tbsp caster (superfine) sugar
1 tsp salt
1 kg / 2 lb 4 oz / 6 ⅔ cups strong white bread flour
a little extra flour, for dusting

Briefly mix together the water, yeast, sugar and salt in a measuring jug; leave to activate for 15 minutes in a warm place. Sit the flour onto a flat work surface and make a well in the middle before pouring the frothy yeast mixture into it. Start to bring the flour into the liquid, mixing until you have a rough ball of dough. Knead the dough firmly for 5–7 minutes until smooth and elastic before placing in a bowl and covering loosely with a tea towel, or a greased piece of cling film. Leave the dough to prove in a warm place until doubled in size; usually 1 hour. Knock the dough back using your hands before shaping into a loaf tin. Leave it to prove for another 30 minutes as you preheat the oven to 180°C (160°C fan) / 350F / gas 4. After the second prove, bake the bread for 25–30 minutes until golden and risen. Remove the dough from the tin and tap on its base; it will sound hollow when it's ready. Allow the loaf to cool before serving.

Simple Pizza Dough

Pizza dough is easy and fun to make at home. It can even be frozen in batches, ready to be defrosted quickly and used in a pinch. Here is a simple recipe to make a batch of dough:

400 g / 14 oz / 2 ⅔ cups strong white bread flour
100 g / 3 ½ oz / ⅔ cup semolina flour (use strong white bread flour if not available)
½ tbsp salt
1 tbsp dried fast-action yeast (or 1 ½ tbsp fresh yeast)
½ tbsp caster (superfine) sugar
300 ml / 10 ½ fl. oz / 1 ½ cups tepid water

Sift the flours and salt onto a flat surface; make a large well in the middle. Mix together the yeast, sugar and water in a jug and leave to one side to get frothy. Pour the mixture into the well and start bringing the flour into the liquid from the edges using a fork. Continue to mix until a rough dough starts to form, at which point you can start to shape the dough with your hands. Knead the dough, stretching it out as you do, using the palm of your hand to push the dough away from the other palm. Repeat this kneading motion for 8–10 minutes until the dough is smooth and elastic. Place the dough in a lightly oiled bowl before covering with a loose piece of cling film or a tea towel. Leave to prove until doubled in size – approximately 45 minutes. Once doubled in size, knead the dough briefly. You can now roll out the dough for pizza bases or freeze it for a later date.

Simple Focaccia

When making focaccia, you can start to incorporate extra ingredients into the dough, such as sun-dried tomato, or herbs like rosemary and thyme. To make a simple focaccia dough, you will need:

450 g / 1 lb / 3 cups strong white bread flour
a little extra flour, for dusting
2 tsp salt
1 ½ tbsp fast-action dried yeast (or 2 ¼ tbsp fresh yeast)
2 tbsp extra-virgin olive oil, plus extra for oiling
350 ml / 12 fl. oz / 1 ½ cups tepid water
1 tbsp flaked sea salt

Combine the flour, salt, yeast, olive oil and 275 ml of the water in a large mixing bowl. Gently, yet firmly, mix together the ingredients until they start to bind into a dough. Knead the dough in the bowl for 4–5 minutes, adding the rest of the reserved water little by little. Stretch the dough out across the bowl before tucking the sides in towards the middle. Turn the bowl 75° to the right and repeat this tucking step for roughly 5 minutes. Turn the dough onto an oiled surface and knead for a further 5 minutes before returning the dough to the bowl; cover loosely and leave to prove until doubled in size. Divide the dough in two and arrange on baking trays, stretching the dough out towards the edges. Leave to prove for another hour. Preheat the oven to 220°C (200°C fan) / 425F / gas 7 and press a little flaked sea salt into the tops of the focaccia dough. Bake for 18–22 minutes until golden and risen.

Simple Ciabatta

A good ciabatta should have a decent crust, coupled with a pleasing chewy texture. For 1 large loaf you will need:

300 g / 10 ½ oz / 2 cups strong white bread flour
1 tsp salt
a little extra flour, for dusting
½ tsp dried fast-action yeast (or ¾ tsp fresh yeast)
200 ml / 7 fl. oz / 1 cup tepid water
2 tbsp olive oil

Mix together the flour, salt and yeast in a food processor and pulse a few times. Turn the motor on, add the olive oil and most of the water, until the dough comes together in a ball; add the remaining water if it's too dry. Turn out the dough and knead for 30 seconds before placing in a bowl and covering; leave to prove for at least 3 hours in a warm place. After proving, transfer the dough carefully to an oiled baking tray, shaping it into an oval loaf with your hands; set to one side to rise for at least another 1 ½ hours. Bake the ciabatta for 40–45 minutes in an oven preheated to 220°C (200°C fan) / 425F / gas 7 until golden and risen, allowing it to cool before serving.

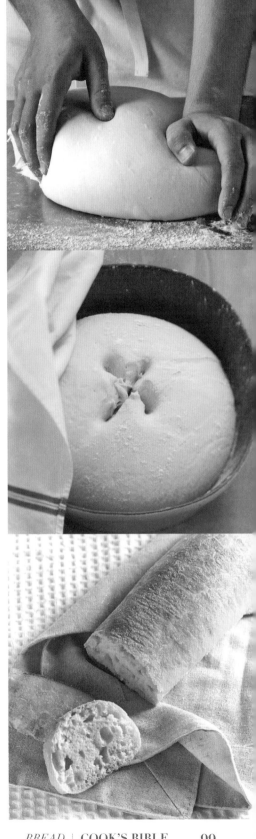

SERVES: **6–8**

PREPARATION TIME: **2 HOURS**

COOKING TIME: **30–35 MINUTES**

INGREDIENTS

500 g / 1 lb 2 oz / 3 ⅓ cups strong
    wholewheat bread flour
a little extra bread flour, for dusting
1 tsp caster (superfine) sugar
1 tsp salt
2 tsp fast-action dried yeast
1 tbsp olive oil, plus extra for greasing
300–350 ml / 10–12 fl. oz / 1 ¼ –1 ½
    cups tepid water

Wholemeal Loaf

1. Combine the flour, sugar, salt
   and yeast in a large mixing bowl
   before working in the olive oil.

2. Add 300 ml of the water and
   mix until a rough dough forms.

3. Add a little more water if it is too
   stiff, then turn out onto a lightly
   floured surface and knead for 8–10
   minutes until smooth and elastic.

4. Place in a large, clean mixing
   bowl and cover with cling film.

5. Leave to rise in a warm place for
   1 hour, or until doubled in size.

6. Grease a 1 ⅓ kg (3 lb) loaf
   tin with a little olive oil.

7. Turn out the dough onto a lightly
   floured surface, then knock it back
   and knead for 2–3 minutes.

8. Shape the dough into the loaf
   tin and cover loosely with an
   oiled piece of cling film; leave
   to rise again for 45 minutes.

9. Preheat the oven to 220°C (200°C
   fan) / 425F / gas 7 and then place
   a small heatproof bowl filled with
   water in the bottom of the oven.

10. Bake the bread for 30–35 minutes
    until risen, then remove from the
    oven and leave to cool for 5 minutes
    before turning out and dusting
    with a little extra flour on top.

MAKES: **12**

PREPARATION TIME: **2 HRS 20 MINUTES**

COOKING TIME: **8–10 MINUTES**

INGREDIENTS

900 g / 2 lb / 6 cups strong white bread flour,
  plus extra for dusting
4 tsp fast-action dried yeast
1 tsp caster (superfine) sugar
1 tsp salt
55 g / 2 oz / ¼ cup unsalted butter, cubed
150 ml / 5 fl. oz / ⅔ cup whole milk, warmed
450 ml / 16 fl. oz / 2 cups lukewarm water

Small Bread Loaves

1. Combine the flour, salt, sugar and dried yeast in a large mixing bowl.

2. Rub the butter into the flour mixture using your fingertips until you have a mixture resembling fine breadcrumbs.

3. Combine the warm milk and water in a jug and pour into the flour mixture, mixing well with a wooden spoon until you have a soft dough.

4. Turn out onto a lightly floured work surface and knead for 8–10 minutes, until you have a smooth, elastic dough.

5. Place the dough in a large mixing bowl and cover with a damp tea towel. Leave to rise in a warm place until doubled in size.

6. Remove the dough from the bowl and knock it down using your hands.

7. Divide the dough into 12 even balls and shape into small loaf shapes.

8. Arrange on oiled baking trays and cover with pieces of oiled cling film, leaving them to prove again in a warm place until doubled in size.

9. Preheat the oven to 220°C (200°C fan) / 425F / gas 7.

10. Remove the cling film and bake the rolls for 8–10 minutes until golden and risen.

11. Remove from the oven when ready and leave them to cool on a wire rack before serving.

SERVES: **4–6**

PREPARATION TIME: **2 HRS 25 MINUTES**

COOKING TIME: **18–22 MINUTES**

INGREDIENTS

450 g / 1 lb / 3 cups strong white bread flour
a little extra flour, for dusting
2 tsp salt
1 ½ tbsp fast-action dried yeast
2 tbsp extra-virgin olive oil, plus extra for
    greasing
350 ml / 12 fl. oz / 1 ½ cups tepid water
75 g / 3 oz / ½ cup sun-dried tomatoes,
    drained and chopped
a few sprigs of rosemary
1 tbsp flaked sea salt

Tomato and Rosemary Focaccia

1. Combine the flour, salt, yeast, olive oil and 275 ml of the water in a large mixing bowl.

2. Gently, yet firmly, stir together the ingredients until they start to bind into a dough.

3. Knead the dough in the bowl for 4–5 minutes, adding the rest of the reserved water little by little.

4. Stretch the dough out across the bowl before tucking the sides in towards the middle.

5. Turn the bowl 75° to the right and repeat this tucking step for roughly 5 minutes.

6. Turn the dough onto an oiled surface and knead for a further 5 minutes, then return the dough to the bowl. Cover loosely and leave to prove until doubled in size.

7. Divide the dough in two and arrange on baking trays, stretching the dough out towards the edges.

8. Leave to prove for another hour.

9. Preheat the oven to 220°C (200°C fan) / 425F / gas 7 and press the rosemary sprigs and sun-dried tomato into the tops of the focaccia dough, creating little punctures on top.

10. Bake for 18–22 minutes until golden and risen.

11. Remove from the oven and sprinkle immediately with flaked sea salt before serving.

MAKES: **1 PIZZA**

PREPARATION TIME: **25–30 MINUTES**

COOKING TIME: **7–9 MINUTES**

INGREDIENTS

300 g / 10 ½ oz / 2 cups strong bread flour,
    plus extra for dusting
1 ½ tsp fast-action dried yeast
1 tsp salt
1 tsp caster (superfine) sugar
1 tbsp olive oil, plus extra for drizzling
200–250 ml/ 7–9 fl. oz / ¾ –1 cup tepid water
200 g / 7 oz / 1 cup passata
150 g / 5 oz / 1 ½ cups grated mozzarella
a few sprigs of basil, to garnish
salt and freshly ground black pepper

Margherita Pizza

1. Combine the flour, yeast, salt and sugar in a large mixing bowl.

2. Add the oil and water and mix until you have a rough dough. Turn out onto a floured surface and knead for 6–8 minutes until smooth and elastic.

3. Cover and leave to rest for at least 15 minutes.

4. Preheat the oven to 240°C (220°C fan) / 475F / gas 9 and place a baking tray, or pizza stone, in the oven to preheat.

5. Turn out the dough and split in half before kneading one

piece briefly. You can freeze the other piece for another time.

6. Roll out on a lightly floured surface into a 25–30 cm (10–12 in) round.

7. Remove the tray or stone from the oven and transfer the dough to it. Working quickly, top with the passata and mozzarella, then drizzle with olive oil.

8. Bake for 7–9 minutes until the base is golden and the cheese is melted and golden.

9. Garnish with basil sprigs before serving.

SERVES: **4**

PREPARATION TIME: **15 MINUTES**

COOKING TIME: **35–40 MINUTES**

INGREDIENTS

750 ml / 1 pint 6 fl. oz / 3 cups whole milk

110 g / 4 oz / ⅔ cup soft light brown sugar

1 tsp ground cinnamon

4 small eggs

1 medium white brioche loaf (ideally 2–3 days old), cut into 2 cm (1 in) thick slices

150 g / 5 oz / ⅔ cup unsalted butter, softened

150 g / 5 oz / 1 cup dried apricots, roughly chopped

Apricot Bread and Butter Pudding

1. Combine the milk, brown sugar and ground cinnamon in a saucepan and heat over a moderate heat, stirring well, to help the sugar dissolve.

2. Remove from the heat and cool to one side for 5 minutes.

3. Whisk the eggs in a heatproof bowl, then pour the warm milk over them, whisking well to incorporate.

4. Preheat the oven to 190°C (170°C fan) / 375F / gas 5. Butter the inside of a 30 cm x 15 cm (12 in x 6 in) heatproof baking dish with 50 g of

the softened butter. Spread the bread with the remaining butter.

5. Arrange a few apricots on the base of the dish, then top with the slices of bread, layering to fit if necessary.

6. Pour over the milk and egg mixture and tuck the remaining apricots in and around the bread.

7. Bake for 35–40 minutes until the tops are crisp.

8. Remove from the oven and leave to rest for 5 minutes before serving.

SERVES: **6**

PREPARATION TIME: **15 MINUTES**

COOKING TIME: **35–45 MINUTES**

INGREDIENTS

175 ml / 6 fl. oz / ¾ cup whole milk
175 ml / 6 fl. oz / ¾ cup double (heavy) cream
3 medium egg yolks
3 medium eggs
110 g / 4 oz / ½ cup caster (superfine) sugar
2 tbsp plain (all purpose) flour
1 tbsp unsalted butter, softened
350 g / 12 oz / 2 ⅓ cups black cherries, pitted
2 large slices of white sandwich bread (ideally 2–3 days old), cut into cubes
2 tbsp Demerara sugar

Cherry Bread Pudding

1. Preheat the oven to 180°C (160°C fan) / 350F / gas 4.

2. Prepare a batter by combining the milk and cream in a saucepan and bringing to a simmer.

3. Remove from the heat and leave to cool to one side for a few minutes.

4. In a large bowl, whisk together the egg yolks and eggs until light and frothy.

5. Add the sugar and whisk until well blended.

6. Fold in the flour, then gradually whisk in the milk and cream mixture.

7. Grease a rectangular baking dish with butter, the pour in the batter.

8. Dot with cherries, bread cubes and half of the demerara sugar, then bake for 35–45 minutes until golden on top.

9. Remove from the oven and sprinkle with the remaining demerara sugar before serving.

MEAT

Roasting Meat

Roasting meat can be an effective and simple way to tackle larger joints of beef, lamb and pork, or when preparing food for a large meal. Often recipes call for roasting meat initially at a high temperature to promote browning and a crust before reducing the temperature to cook the inside evenly. Cooking at lower temperature tends to preserve juices and thus give more tender and tasty results. Depending on the kind of meat you are roasting, the cooking temperatures and method will vary. For example, if you are roasting a rib of beef, you will want to start it off at a higher temperature for 15 minutes before reducing the temperature to cook the inside evenly. However, if you were roasting a pork shoulder in the oven, you would want to roast it at a lower temperature for a longer time to help give you the best results because pork shoulder is more conducive to this method.

When roasting any kind of meat, it is important to remember that you should let the meat come up to room temperature before roasting for best results; remove meat from the fridge and let it stand for anywhere between 10–30 minutes (depending on size) at room temperature before roasting. Always season meat generously before cooking and make sure that your oven is fully preheated before roasting in order to achieve best results.

Braising Meat

When it comes to braising, most meat generally benefits from sealing before being braised in liquid. This helps the meat to retain juices that would otherwise be lost without the action of sealing. Certain cuts of meat are prime candidates for braising owing to their composition. For example, a piece of beef such as oxtail needs to be braised in liquid for a long time in order to help break down the sinews and collagen. The same goes for a cut of lamb, such as the shoulder. Braising meat can be a really simple way to make delicious, cost-effective dishes by utilising cheaper cuts of meat. The principle remains the same with all kinds of braising; season and seal the meat in hot oil. Drain any excess fat before covering the meat with liquid, such as stock. The liquid is brought to a simmer before being covered and simmered on the stove over a low temperature, or in the oven at approximately 150°C (130°C fan) / 300F / gas 2. After a couple of hours the meat should be easy to pull apart with your fingers – a classic sign that the meat is ready.

Baking Meat

Baking meat follows similar principles to roasting, but can usually be done on a smaller scale. Minced meat is a good candidate for baking as the fat content helps to prevent the meat from drying out. A classic example of baking meat would be in meatballs where minced meat is scrunched together with seasonings, breadcrumbs and occasionally an egg, before being shaped into balls on a baking tray. The meatballs are then baked in a moderate oven until golden on the outside and juicy within.

Stewing Meat

Stewing meat is very similar to braising, except that where braising tends to be appropriate for large, single pieces of meat, stewing is ideal for smaller pieces of meat, such as diced stewing steak, or shoulder of lamb. As with braising, it is a good idea to seal the pieces of meat in hot oil before covering them in liquid and simmering over a low heat until tender.

Grilling Meat

Grilling meat is a good way to quickly and healthily prepare cuts of steak, lamb, or pork. Preheating your grill to a moderately high temperature allows the meat to cook quickly, but also evenly. As an example, lightly coat a pork chop in a little oil before seasoning generously. Grill for 4–5 minutes on both sides, depending on thickness, until the meat is firm with a little spring to the touch.

Frying Meat

When cooking cuts of meat that can be served at different cooking degrees (e.g. rare, medium, well-done), pan-frying lets you retain more control in the process than any other method. It is also one of the quickest methods to cook meat as the meat is fried in hot oil for a sustained period of time, thus expediting the cooking time. Remember to avoid overcrowding a pan when frying meat otherwise it will stew rather than fry.

SERVES: **6–8**

PREPARATION TIME: **10 MINUTES**

COOKING TIME: **1 ½–1 ¾ HOURS**

INGREDIENTS

1.80 kg / 4 lb leg of lamb, trimmed
2 tbsp olive oil
3 sticks of celery, roughly chopped
2 small carrots, roughly chopped
2 bulbs of garlic, halved horizontally
a small handful of mint, finely chopped
salt and freshly ground black pepper

Roasted Leg of Lamb

1. Preheat the oven to 180°C (160°C fan) / 350F / gas 4 and line a roasting tin with aluminium foil.

2. Make a few shallow incisions in the leg of lamb with a sharp knife, then season with salt and pepper.

3. Massage the olive oil into the leg and set it to one side.

4. Arrange the celery, carrot and garlic in the base of the roasting tin and sit the leg of lamb on top.

5. Roast the lamb for 1 ½–1 ¾ hours depending on desired cooking degree. As a guideline, the meat should register 60°C / 140F on a meat thermometer for medium.

6. Remove the lamb from the oven and sprinkle with mint.

7. Leave to rest for at least 15 minutes, covered loosely with aluminium foil, before serving.

INGREDIENTS

3 medium aubergines (eggplants), cut into
   1 cm (½ in) thick slices
2 tbsp olive oil
2 large onions
2 cloves of garlic, minced
450 g / 1 lb / 3 cups lamb mince
2 tsp dried oregano
½ tsp ground cinnamon
400 g / 14 oz / 2 cups canned chopped
   tomatoes
225 ml / 8 fl. oz / 1 cup lamb stock
75 g / 3 oz / ⅓ cup unsalted butter
75 g / 3 oz / ½ cup plain (all purpose) flour
750 ml / 1 pint 6 fl. oz / 3 cups whole milk
2 small egg yolks
110 g / 4 oz / 1 cup Cheddar, grated
a few sprigs of thyme, to garnish
salt and pepper

Moussaka

1. Salt the slices of aubergine and arrange on kitchen paper to drain; pat dry after 10 minutes.

2. Slice one onion and finely chop the other; heat the oil in a large casserole dish set over a medium heat and sauté the chopped onion and garlic for 4–5 minutes.

3. Add the lamb mince and brown all over before stirring in the dried herbs and spices.

4. Add the chopped tomatoes and lamb stock and bring to a simmer before cooking for 30 minutes over a reduced heat.

5. Preheat the oven to 180°C (160°C fan) / 350F / gas 4.

6. Melt the butter in a large saucepan set over a moderate heat; whisk in the flour to make a roux and cook until golden.

7. Whisk in the milk in a slow, steady stream until thickened; simmer for 5 minutes before whisking in the egg yolks, cheese and seasoning.

8. Spoon a little of the lamb sauce into the base of a 20 cm (8 in) square baking dish before topping with a layer of aubergine slices.

9. Spoon some of the cheese sauce onto one side of the dish, spooning the lamb sauce on the other side.

10. Tuck the remaining slices of aubergine into the dish, spooning any of the remaining sauces on top and around.

11. Top with the sliced onion before baking for 40–50 minutes, until golden brown on top and piping hot in the middle; serve garnished with thyme sprigs.

INGREDIENTS

1.6 kg / 3 lb 9 oz topside of beef
2 tbsp sunflower oil
salt and freshly ground black pepper

Roast Beef

1. Preheat the oven to 190°C (170°C fan) / 375F / gas 5.

2. Place a trivet in a roasting tin and set to one side.

3. Tie the piece of topside with kitchen string, at 4 cm (1 ½ in) intervals, to secure.

4. Season with salt and pepper and leave to stand for 5 minutes.

5. Heat the oil in a large sauté pan set over a moderate heat until very hot.

6. Seal the beef in the hot oil until golden brown all over, then carefully remove to the trivet.

7. Roast for 50–55 minutes for rare and a further 10–20 minutes for medium to well done.

8. Remove from the oven and leave to rest, covered loosely with aluminium foil, for at least 20 minutes before slicing and serving.

SERVES: **4**

PREPARATION TIME: **35–40 MINUTES**

COOKING TIME: **40–45 MINUTES**

INGREDIENTS

2 tbsp olive oil
1 onion, finely chopped
1 stick of celery, finely chopped
2 medium courgettes (zucchinis), sliced
500 g / 1 lb 2 oz / 3 ⅓ cups beef mince
1 tsp Worcestershire sauce
225 ml / 8 fl. oz / 1 cup beef stock
1 kg / 2 lb 4 oz / 6 ⅔ cups floury potatoes,
   peeled and diced evenly
75 g / 3 oz / ⅓ cup unsalted butter, softened
75 g / 3 oz / ¾ cup Parmesan, grated
salt and pepper

Beef and Courgette Cottage Pie

1. Heat the olive oil in a large casserole dish set over a moderate heat until hot.

2. Sauté the onion and celery for 4–5 minutes, stirring occasionally.

3. Add the sliced courgettes and continue to cook for 3–4 minutes.

4. Add the beef mince and brown all over, then add the Worcestershire sauce and beef stock.

5. Bring to a simmer and cook over a reduced heat for 20–25 minutes.

6. Meanwhile, cook the potatoes in a large saucepan of boiling, salted water for 15–20 minutes, until tender.

7. Drain and leave to steam dry for a few minutes before mashing with the butter, until smooth. Adjust the seasoning to taste.

8. Preheat the oven to 180°C (160°C fan) / 350F / gas 4 and spoon the beef and courgette mixture into the base of a 20 cm x 10 cm x 5 cm (8 in x 4 in x 2 in) baking dish.

9. Spread the mashed potato

on top and sprinkle over the Parmesan, then bake for 40–45 minutes until golden on top.

10. Remove from the oven and leave to stand for a few minutes before serving.

SERVES: **6–8**

PREPARATION TIME: **20 MINUTES**

COOKING TIME: **25–30 MINUTES**

INGREDIENTS

2 x 700 g / 1 lb 12 oz pork fillets
2 tbsp Dijon mustard
2 tbsp demerara sugar
2 tbsp sunflower oil
a large handful of mixed lettuce leaves,
    to garnish
salt and freshly ground black pepper

Roast Pork

1. Preheat the oven to 190°C (170°C fan) / 375F / gas 5.

2. Trim the fillets of any excess fat, or silver skin using a sharp knife.

3. Mix together the mustard and sugar, then smear all over the pork fillets. Season well.

4. Sit the pork fillets on trivets sat inside a roasting tin, then drizzle with oil.

5. Roast for 25–30 minutes until a meat thermometer registers 63–65°C / 145–150F.

6. Remove from the oven and leave to rest for at least 10 minutes, covered loosely with aluminium foil.

7. Slice and serve with the lettuce on the side.

SERVES: **4**

PREPARATION TIME: **20 MINUTES**

COOKING TIME: **10–15 MINUTES**

INGREDIENTS

4 x 250 g / 9 oz boneless pork chops
2 tbsp olive oil
1 tbsp balsamic vinegar
½ iceberg lettuce, chopped
1 lemon, cut into wedges
a few sprigs of oregano, chopped
a few sprigs of rosemary, chopped
salt and freshly ground black pepper

Grilled Pork Chops

1. Preheat your grill to hot and line a grilling tray with aluminium foil.

2. Trim any excess fat from the pork chops and drizzle with oil and balsamic vinegar and season generously.

3. Arrange on the tray and grill for 5–7 minutes on both sides until a meat thermometer registers 63–65°C / 145–150F.

4. Remove the chops from the grill and leave to rest for at least 5 minutes, then sprinkle with the chopped herbs.

5. Serve with the lettuce and lemon wedges on the side.

SERVES: **4**

PREPARATION TIME: **15–20 MINUTES**

COOKING TIME: **25–30 MINUTES**

INGREDIENTS

700 g / 1 lb 12 oz piece of venison fillet, trimmed
2 tbsp sunflower oil
5 ripe pears, halved and cored
1 tbsp apricot jam (jelly), warmed
a few strawberries, hulled and chopped
200 g / 7 oz / 1 ½ cups red grapes
2 tbsp balsamic vinegar
salt and pepper

Venison Fillet with Roasted Fruit

1. Preheat the oven to 190°C (170°C fan) / 375F / gas 5.

2. Finely chop one of the pears, keeping the remaining pears in halves.

3. Rub the venison fillet with oil and season generously. Heat a sauté pan over a moderate heat until hot.

4. Seal the fillet until golden brown all over and remove from the heat. Pat dry and brush with the jam.

5. Press the chopped pear and strawberry on top of the fillet

and arrange the pear halves and grapes in the roasting tray.

6. Drizzle with balsamic vinegar, then sit the venison fillet on top.

7. Roast for 15–20 minutes until a meat thermometer registers 55–57°C / 130–135F before removing just the venison from the oven, leaving the fruit to continue roasting.

8. Let the venison rest, covered loosely with aluminium foil, for at least 10 minutes.

9. Remove the fruit from the oven once the venison has rested. Slice the venison fillet and serve with roast fruit and any accumulated juices.

SERVES: **8**

PREPARATION TIME: **45 MINUTES**

COOKING TIME: **1 ¾–2 ¼ HOURS**

INGREDIENTS

150 g / 5 oz / 1 cup kumquats
a few sprigs of rosemary
2 kg / 5 lb 7 oz piece of gammon,
   trimmed and soaked in cold water
   for at least 24 hours
110 g / 4 oz / ½ cup orange marmalade
2 tbsp sunflower oil
salt and freshly ground black pepper

Marmalade Roast Gammon

1. Preheat the oven to 200°C
   (180°C fan) / 400F / gas 6 and
   place the kumquats and rosemary
   in the base of a roasting tin.

2. Drain the gammon, then pat
   dry and tie with kitchen string,
   at 3 cm (1 ½ in) intervals.

3. Rub the gammon with the
   marmalade and season generously,
   then sit on top of the kumquats.

4. Drizzle with the oil and roast in
   the oven for 10 minutes. Lower

   the temperature to 180°C
   (160°C fan) / 350F / gas 4.

5. Roast for 1 ¾ –2 ¼ hours until
   the gammon registers 65-70°C /
   150-158F on a meat thermometer.

6. Remove from the oven and leave
   to rest for at least 30 minutes,
   covered loosely with aluminium foil.

7. Serve warm, or cold with the
   kumquats on the side.

SERVES: **4**

PREPARATION TIME: **15 MINUTES**

COOKING TIME: **1 ¾–2 HOURS**

INGREDIENTS

1.2 kg / 2 lb 10 oz / 5 cups stewing
   steak, cut into ½ cm (1 in) cubes
55 ml / 2 fl. oz / ¼ cup sunflower oil
3 large carrots, peeled and sliced
110 ml / 4 fl. oz / ½ cup red wine
850 ml / 1 pint 10 fl. oz / 3 ½ cups beef
   stock
a small handful of flat-leaf parsley, finely
   chopped
salt and pepper

Beef and Carrot Stew

1. Season the stewing steak
generously with salt and pepper
as you heat a casserole dish over
a moderate heat until hot.

2. Add a little oil to the dish and
seal the steak, in batches, until
golden brown all over.

3. Remove the sealed steak to a
plate and reduce the heat a little
before adding the carrots.

4. Sauté for 3–4 minutes, stirring
occasionally, before adding
the steak back to the dish.

5. Add the wine and let it bubble
and reduce by half before
covering with the stock.

6. Bring to a simmer and cook
over a reduced heat, covered,
for 1 ¾–2 hours until the beef
is tender and you can pull it
apart with your fingers.

7. Adjust the seasoning to taste before
ladling into serving bowls and
garnishing with chopped parsley.

SERVES: **6**

PREPARATION TIME: **15 MINUTES**

COOKING TIME: **45–50 MINUTES**

INGREDIENTS

55 ml / 2 fl. oz / ¼ cup olive oil
1 stick of cinnamon
2 large onions, roughly chopped
2 carrots, peeled and chopped
1 red pepper, deseeded and chopped
2 cloves of garlic, chopped
2 tsp ground cumin
1 tsp ground coriander
1 tsp paprika
1 tsp chilli (chili) powder
750 g / 1 lb 10 oz / 5 cups beef mince
600 g / 1 lb 5 oz / 3 cups canned
    chopped tomatoes
400 g / 14 oz / 2 cups canned kidney
    beans, drained
250 ml / 9 fl. oz / 1 cup beef stock
flour tortillas, to serve
salt and pepper

Chilli con Carne

1. Heat the olive oil in a large casserole dish set over a moderate heat.

2. Add the cinnamon and fry for a few seconds before adding the chopped vegetables and garlic.

3. Sauté for 7–8 minutes, until lightly browned before adding the ground spices.

4. Stir well and cook for 1 minute before adding the beef mince.

5. Cook the mince until browned all over before adding the chopped tomatoes, kidney beans and stock.

6. Bring the mixture to a simmer before reducing the heat and cooking for 45–50 minutes.

7. Adjust the seasoning to taste before serving with flour tortillas.

Making Burgers

Burgers can be made from beef, pork, or lamb mince. There are more exotic versions, such as venison and bison as well, should you wish to try something a bit different.

An important rule when preparing burgers is to make sure your mince has a high enough fat content in order to help the burgers retain moisture and taste. Look to buy mince with 20% fat content for best results although healthier, tasty versions can be made with leaner mince. Seasoning the meat with salt before mixing will help your burgers to hold their shape.

Before cooking, make a small imprint in the middle of the patties with your thumb – this will help them retain a flat shape as they cook.

SERVES: **4**

PREPARATION TIME: **30 MINUTES**

COOKING TIME: **15–20 MINUTES**

INGREDIENTS

600 g / 1 lb 5 oz / 4 cups beef mince
  (at least 20% fat)
350 g / 12 oz / 3 cups frozen oven chips
2 medium onions
2 tbsp olive oil
4 rashers of back bacon
110 g / 4 oz / ½ cup barbecue sauce, or
  tomato ketchup
4 sesame seed burger buns, split
a large handful of frissee lettuce, to
  garnish
salt and freshly ground black pepper

Bacon and Onion Hamburger

1. Scrunch the beef mince with plenty of seasoning in a large mixing bowl, then cover and chill for 10 minutes.

2. Preheat the oven to 200°C (180°C fan) / 400F / gas 6, then spread the fries on a baking tray and set to one side.

3. Divide the beef mince into 4 even balls and shape into patties between your hands.

4. Arrange on a baking tray, spaced apart, then press a thumb imprint into the middle of each patty.

5. Bake the burgers and fries simultaneously for 15–20 minutes until the burgers are firm, yet springy to the touch and the fries are golden brown and cooked through.

6. While the burgers are baking, preheat the grill to hot.

7. Heat the olive oil in a large frying pan set over a moderate heat and sauté the onions with a little salt for 7–8 minutes, until golden and soft.

8. Grill the bacon for 2–3 minutes on both sides, then remove and pat dry.

9. To build your burgers, spread a little barbecue sauce or ketchup onto the bun bottoms and sit a patty on top.

10. Top with onions and bacon before placing the tops of the buns in place.

11. Serve with fries and lettuce on the side.

POULTRY

AND BIRDS

Preparing to Roast

When preparing any kind of poultry for roasting, take time and care to wash the bird thoroughly, inside and out. Remove any giblets and excess fat from the cavity before removing the wingtips with a sharp knife (these can be reserved for making gravy or stock). Thoroughly pat the bird dry and remove any hairs. Removing the wishbone from a whole bird will also help with carving after roasting. For a chicken, find the top of the bone using your finger – it should be located at the top of the breast near the base of the neck. Use your paring knife to cut down and around the bones that protrude from the tip of the wishbone. Once they are loosened away from the flesh, snap the bone up and away from the bird and twist to remove. Turkeys and ducks have wishbones that are anatomically slightly different. The process for removing them is the same, although they may sit differently than they do in chicken. As long as you separate the two bones away from the tip of the wishbone and the flesh, it should be easy to cut out.

Most kinds of poultry benefit from being trussed – tied with kitchen string to help a bird keep its shape and cook more evenly during roasting. Some smaller birds, such as poussin, don't need to be trussed. Anything as large, or larger than a guinea fowl would benefit from trussing. For an average-sized chicken, take approximately 1 m (3 ft) of kitchen string. Place the chicken on its breast with its legs facing towards you. Start with the middle of your piece of string under the tailbone of the chicken, then wrap each end once around a leg and cross the string over in the middle. Pull the ends of the string firmly to bring the legs inwards towards the body. At this point, take each end of the string away from you towards the head of the bird, looping it around the front of the chicken, over the wings. Keeping the string held taut, turn the chicken over and tie a secure knot just under the neck bone. Now that your bird is trussed, you can trim any excess string before seasoning and roasting.

Roasting

Having trussed your bird, rub it with oil, or butter and season with plenty of salt and pepper. A small orange, apple, or lemon can be placed in the cavity of the bird (size allowing) in order to keep it as moist as possible as it roasts. Additional seasoning, such as fresh herbs can be placed between the skin and flesh, or inside the cavity. Place your trussed bird on a roasting tray and roast in an oven preheated to 190°C (170°C fan) / 375F / gas 5. A 1.5 kg / 3 lb 5 oz chicken, will need approximately 1 hour and 15–20 minutes in the oven. As a general rule of thumb, roast your poultry for 20 minutes per 450 g / 1 lb of weight plus an additional 10–15 minutes. To check if the chicken is ready, take a reading of the thickest part of the thigh with a meat thermometer; once the chicken reads 74°C / 165F, it's ready. Remove it from the oven and leave it to rest, covered loosely with foil, for 15 minutes to help it retain its juices before carving.

SERVES: **4**

PREPARATION TIME: **20 MINUTES**

COOKING TIME: **1 HOUR 20 MINUTES**

INGREDIENTS

1.6 kg / 3 lb 9 oz chicken, cleaned with
   wishbone removed
1 small orange, or satsuma
1 small apple
1 tbsp olive oil
1 tbsp unsalted butter, softened
a small bunch of thyme sprigs
6 shallots, halved
8 chipolatas
8 rashers of streaky bacon
salt and freshly ground black pepper

Roast Chicken with Sausages

1. Preheat the oven to 190°C (170°C fan) / 375F / gas 5.

2. Stuff the cavity of the bird with the orange and apple, then rub with the oil and butter and season generously.

3. Arrange the thyme and shallots in a roasting tin and sit the chicken on top.

4. Roast for 1 hour. Meanwhile, wrap the chipolatas with the streaky bacon and chill.

5. After 1 hour, add the wrapped chipolatas to the chicken and continue to cook for a further 15–20 minutes until the chicken is ready.

6. To check, pierce the thickest part of the thigh. If the juices run clear, it is ready.

7. Alternatively, check with a meat thermometer; if the thigh registers at least 70°C / 160F, it is ready.

8. Remove from the oven and leave to rest, covered loosely with foil, for 10 minutes before serving.

SERVES: 4

PREPARATION TIME: 20 MINUTES

COOKING TIME: 1 HOUR 20 MINUTES

INGREDIENTS

1.6 kg / 3 lb 9 oz chicken, cleaned with
    wishbone removed, legs trussed
1 small orange, or satsuma
1 small apple
2 tbsp olive oil
1 tbsp unsalted butter, softened
5 medium red onions, halved
5 shallots, halved
150 g / 5 oz / 1 cup baby plum tomatoes
75 g / 3 oz / ½ cup Kalamata olives, pitted
    and halved
2 slices of sourdough bread, cubed
2 tbsp cottage cheese, or queso fresco
salt and freshly ground black pepper

Roast Chicken with Onions

1. Preheat the oven to 190°C (170°C fan) / 375F / gas 5.

2. Stuff the cavity of the bird with the orange and apple and rub with 1 tbsp of the oil and the butter. Season generously.

3. Arrange the onions, shallots, tomatoes and olives in a roasting tin, then drizzle with the remaining oil and season.

4. After an hour of cooking, add the bread cubes to the baking tray.

5. Sit the chicken on top and roast for 1–1 ¼ hours. To check, pierce the thickest part of the thigh. If the juices run clear, it is ready.

6. Alternatively, check with a meat thermometer; if the thigh registers at least 70°C / 160F, it is ready.

7. Remove from the oven and leave to rest, covered loosely with foil, for 10 minutes.

8. Spoon the cottage cheese around the chicken before serving.

SERVES: **8**

PREPARATION TIME: **45 MINUTES**

COOKING TIME: **2–2 ½ HOURS**

INGREDIENTS

2.7 kg / 6 lb turkey, cleaned with
    wishbone removed
55 g / 2 oz / ¼ cup unsalted butter,
    softened
300 g / 10 ½ oz / 4 cups mixed wild
    mushrooms
½ small onion, finely chopped
1 tsp dried thyme
a large bunch of flat-leaf parsley, finely
    chopped
salt and freshly ground black pepper

Turkey with Roast Mushrooms

1. Preheat the oven to 190°C
   (170°C fan) / 375F / gas 5.

2. Smear the turkey with the
   butter, season generously
   and sit in a roasting tin.

3. Roast for 1 ¾ hours, then
   remove from the oven.

4. Toss together the mushrooms, onion
   and thyme and arrange around
   the turkey in the roasting tin.

5. Return to the oven for 30–45
   minutes until the turkey is cooked.

6. To check, pierce the thickest
   part of the thigh. If the juices
   run clear, it is ready.

7. Alternatively, check with a meat
   thermometer. If the thigh registers
   at least 70°C / 160F, it is ready.

8. Remove from the oven and
   sprinkle immediately with parsley.

9. Leave to rest, covered loosely with
   foil, for 30 minutes before serving.

SERVES: **4**

PREPARATION TIME: **10–15 MINUTES**

COOKING TIME: **55–60 MINUTES**

INGREDIENTS

150 g / 5 oz / 1 cup pearl onions, peeled
2 medium red onions, quartered
4 small parsnips, peeled
4 medium carrots, peeled and halved
1 courgette (zucchini), sliced
55 ml / 2 fl. oz / ¼ cup sunflower oil
4 x guinea fowl legs, trimmed and cleaned
250 ml / 9 fl. oz / 1 cup chicken stock
1 tbsp chicken gravy granules
salt and freshly ground black pepper

Guinea Fowl with Roast Vegetables

1. Preheat the oven to 190°C (170°C fan) / 375F / gas 5.

2. Toss together the vegetables with the oil and a little seasoning, then arrange in a roasting tin.

3. Roast for 10 minutes, then remove from the oven.

4. Season the guinea fowl legs and sit on top of the vegetables.

5. Return to the oven for 45–50 minutes until the legs are golden brown and cooked through.

6. Remove from the oven and leave to rest, covered loosely with foil, for 10 minutes.

7. Meanwhile, bring the chicken stock to the boil in a small saucepan set over a moderate heat.

8. Whisk in the gravy granules, cooking until the gravy thickens. Adjust the seasoning to taste.

9. Serve the roast vegetables with the guinea fowl and gravy on top.

Jointing

Jointing poultry is a useful skill to learn. Breaking a bird down into pieces will allow you to buy whole birds, which is cheaper than buying the separate pieces. It also allows you use different parts of a bird for different recipes. Chicken legs and thighs are ideal for a hearty French stew, such as coq au vin, whereas the breast would be better served, for example, pan-fried with a little tarragon and cream to finish. Even though it is easy to buy the separate pieces in supermarkets, it is still a valuable skill to have.

Before attempting to joint a bird, make sure that your knife is well sharpened. A combination of a paring knife and a 18 cm (7 in) chef's knife is ideal. If the bird still has its wingtips intact, find the knuckle of the joint and cut through it with your knife. Remove the tailbone, or Parson's nose, as it is known and discard. Cut through the skin between the thighs and the body of the chicken to expose the hip joint. Take your knife around the back of the legs, towards the back of the bird and start to ease the leg out its joint using your hands. Use your knife to cut through the joint to separate the legs from the body. To remove the wishbone of a chicken, now that you have the body left, run your knife carefully down either side of the centre of the breast to separate the breast from the ribcage. Follow your knife around the shape of the ribcage until the breasts are mostly separated. Once you can see the shoulder knuckle, cut through it to separate the breasts. The carcass can be used to make stock, or broken down into pieces to make gravy. Make sure to trim and clean your jointed pieces before cooking them.

Frying Poultry

Poultry can be fried either with the skin on, or as skinless pieces. Before frying, pat the pieces dry and season with salt and pepper. Heat a generous tablespoon of oil in a non-stick frying pan set over a moderate heat. Once the oil is hot, add the poultry to the pan, skin side down, making sure not to overcrowd. Leave the pieces untouched until a golden-brown seal develops underneath. Flip and cook the other sides until the pieces feel firm with a very slight spring to the touch – cooked pieces of poultry will be uniformly white inside, with no visible trace of pink.

Owing to this quick method of cooking, it is advisable to fry poultry breasts rather than the legs or thighs, which are better suited to braising or baking.

Grilling Poultry

As with frying, grilling poultry is best reserved for when you use pieces of the breast, rather than the legs, or thighs. Preheat your grill to hot, then rub the breasts with a little oil and season with salt and pepper. Arrange spaced apart on a grilling tray and cook for 4–5 minutes on both sides until they feel firm to the touch, with a very slight spring. Grilled poultry will be uniformly white throughout with no trace of pink when cooked through. Grilling is also a great way to cook smaller birds that have been spatchcocked. To spatchcock a poussin, or small chicken, clean and trim the bird. Remove the wishbone and cut out the spine using a sharp pair of poultry shears. Flatten out the bird on a chopping board, then season and grill until the thickest part of the thigh registers 74°C / 165F on a meat thermometer.

Baking Poultry

Baking is a great way to cook several legs, or thighs of poultry, especially if the pieces are bone-in. The bone helps to conduct heat and produce evenly cooked pieces of meat. You can also bake poultry breasts, which is ideal for when you need to cook more than 2, or 3 pieces at once. Preheat your oven to 180°C (160°C fan) / 350F / gas 4 and arrange the pieces on a baking tray, or in roasting tin. Drizzle with oil and season with salt and pepper before baking for 35–45 minutes, depending on their size. To check if they are cooked, pierce the thickest part of a thigh or leg; its juices will run clear when ready. If you are still not sure, check with a meat thermometer – the pieces should read at least 74°C / 165F.

Minced Poultry

Minced poultry, such as turkey, or chicken, can be ideal for making healthier versions of classics, such as meatballs, burgers and even Bolognaise. As poultry tends to have a lower fat content compared to minced meat, you should add an egg to your ingredients when preparing meatballs, or burgers with turkey, or chicken mince. Minced poultry can either be baked, fried, or grilled depending on the recipe you are preparing. For a quick chicken burger using mince, bind together 450 g / 1 lb / 3 cups of chicken mince in a bowl with 1 large egg, a large handful of breadcrumbs, some chopped parsley and seasoning. Chill the mixture for 15 minutes then divide and shape into patties. Arrange on a baking tray and press a thumb into their middles to make a small imprint. Bake for 20–25 minutes until golden brown and cooked through before serving in buns.

SERVES: **4**

PREPARATION TIME: **10 MINUTES**

COOKING TIME: **45–55 MINUTES**

INGREDIENTS

3 shallots, halved
1 red pepper, deseeded and chopped
2 medium floury potatoes, peeled and
    cut into wedges
6 anchovy fillets, drained and sliced
4 x medium skinless chicken breasts,
    trimmed
225 g / 8 oz / 1 cup passata
150 ml / 5 fl. oz / ⅔ cup red wine
110 g / 4 oz / ⅔ cup black olives, pitted
55 ml / 2 fl. oz / ¼ cup olive oil
1 lemon, zested
a small bunch of flat-leaf parsley,
    chopped
salt and freshly ground black pepper

Chicken Cacciatore

1. Preheat the oven to 180°C
(160°C fan) / 350F / gas 4.

2. Arrange the shallots, pepper,
potatoes and anchovy fillets in
a large, round baking dish.

3. Tuck in the chicken breasts then
pour the passata and red
wine around the chicken.

4. Dot the black olives around the
dish, then drizzle everything with
olive oil. Season generously and
scatter over the lemon zest.

5. Bake for 45–55 minutes until
the chicken is cooked through
and the potatoes are soft.

6. Garnish with chopped
parsley before serving.

SERVES: **4**

PREPARATION TIME: **5 MINUTES**

COOKING TIME: **10 MINUTES**

INGREDIENTS

2 tbsp groundnut oil
4 x small skinless chicken breasts, cut
　　into strips
300 g / 10 ½ oz / 2 cups prawns
　　(shrimp), peeled and deveined with
　　tails intact
1 small head of white cabbage,
　　shredded
2 tbsp soy sauce
1 tbsp fish sauce
1 tbsp rice wine vinegar
1 tbsp sesame seeds
a small handful of coriander (cilantro)
　　leaves
1 lemon, cut into wedges
salt and freshly ground black pepper

Chicken and Prawn Stir-fry

1. Heat the groundnut oil in a large wok set over a high heat until hot.

2. Season the chicken strips and prawns and flash-fry for 2 minutes, stirring and tossing occasionally.

3. Remove to a plate and add the cabbage to the wok. Cook over a slightly reduced heat, covered, for 2 minutes.

4. Remove the cover and return the chicken, prawns and any accumulated juices to the wok.

5. Stir-fry for a further 2–3 minutes until the chicken and prawns are cooked through.

6. Season the stir-fry with soy sauce, fish sauce and rice wine vinegar before dividing between dishes.

7. Garnish with a sprinkling of sesame seeds and coriander leaves, serving with the lemon wedges on the side.

SERVES: **4**

PREPARATION TIME: **10 MINUTES**

COOKING TIME: **20–25 MINUTES**

INGREDIENTS

600 g / 1 lb 5 oz / 4 cups turkey mince
110 g / 4 oz / 1 cup dried breadcrumbs
1 large egg, beaten
a small bunch of coriander (cilantro),
  finely chopped
1 tbsp fish sauce
2 tbsp dark soy sauce, plus extra for
  serving
2 tbsp sunflower oil
freshly ground black pepper

Turkey and Herb Meatballs

1. Preheat the oven to 190°C (170°C fan) / 375F / gas 5 and line a large baking tray with greaseproof paper.

2. Scrunch together the turkey mince, breadcrumbs, egg, coriander, fish sauce, soy sauce and pepper in a large mixing bowl.

3. Take generous tablespoons of the mixture and shape into meatballs

between your hands, then arrange, spaced apart, on the baking tray.

4. Drizzle with the oil and bake for 20–25 minutes until golden brown all over.

5. Remove from the oven and serve with small dishes of soy sauce for dipping.

SERVES: **4**

PREPARATION TIME: **I HR 20 MINUTES**

COOKING TIME: **15–20 MINUTES**

INGREDIENTS

675 g / I lb 10 oz / 4 ½ cups plain (all purpose)
 flour, plus extra for rolling
450 g / I lb / 2 cups table salt
5 medium egg whites
450 ml / 16 fl. oz / 2 cups cold water
450 g / I lb / 3 cups baby potatoes
2 x large duck breasts, trimmed and cleaned
225 g / 8 oz / 2 cups salad onions
2 tbsp olive oil
salt and freshly ground black pepper

Duck Breast in Salt Crust

1. Combine the flour, salt, egg whites and water in a mixing bowl until a dough forms. Knead briefly to smooth out, then cover and chill for 1 hour.

2. Parboil the potatoes in a saucepan of salted, boiling water for 15 minutes. Drain and leave to cool to one side. Preheat the oven to 190°C (170°C fan) / 375F / gas 5.

3. Score the skin of the duck breasts in a criss-cross pattern using a sharp knife.

4. Season generously and place skin side down in a cold, heavy-based frying pan.

5. Cook over a medium heat, letting the fat render slowly and the skin crisp until golden brown. Remove the duck breasts from the pan and drain on kitchen paper.

6. Roll out the salt crust dough on a lightly floured surface to ½ cm (¼ in) thickness and divide in two pieces.

7. Sit a duck breast in the middle of each piece of dough and bring the edges over and around the duck.

8. Carefully lift onto a baking tray. Combine the potatoes and salad onions in a roasting tin and drizzle

with olive oil and seasoning. Bake the duck and the vegetables simultaneously for 15–20 minutes.

9. Remove and leave to cool . Crack the crust and serve with the vegetables.

FISH
AND SHELLFISH

Types of Fish

The popularity of fish around the world is almost unparalleled, with international cuisines having signature dishes using fish that are indigenous to their area. From Bouillabaisse in the south of France to cod accras in western Africa and Cullen Skink in the Scottish Highlands, fish's appeal is global. Fish has the benefit of cooking quickly, making it ideal for quick suppers, as well as providing an excellent source of essential fatty acids, protein and nutrients. Fish can be separated into two main categories when looked at from a culinary perspective – round fish and flatfish.

Classic examples of round fish are salmon, cod and haddock. Within the category of round fish, there are various types of fish, with some having different textures and tastes. Pollock and Mackerel differ significantly in taste and texture, but both are round fish. Round fish can be oily in nature, although not every round fish is an oily variety. Fish, such as sea bream and sea bass, are ideal for cooking whole, whereas flatfish varieties aren't as conducive to baking whole. Round fish have two fillets, either side of the backbone.

Flatfish varieties include the soles, such as Dover and lemon, as well as turbot and halibut. The vast majority of flatfish are distinctive in that their skin is darker on the top and whiter underneath. Both turbot and halibut are prized for their firm, white flesh and as such tend to be quite expensive. Dover and lemon sole have delicate flesh with a distinct, almost sweet flavour. Sole Veronique and Sole Bonne Femme are just two classic French dishes that Dover sole has inspired. Lemon sole and plaice are ideal for goujons; pieces of fillet, battered and deep-fried until golden and crisp. Preparing flatfish is a little different to preparing most kinds of round fish; in order to fillet the fish, the skin on the top and bottom needs to be removed before separating the fillets from the bone. Most flatfish have four fillets; two on the top and two on the bottom, compared to the two fillets that round fish have. Even though most round fish are good candidates for whole cooking, size dependent, certain kinds of flatfish, such as Dover sole, can be cooked whole, often under a hot grill.

Skinning Fish

To skin a fish, you will need a sharp filleting knife. A good filleting knife is slightly flexible, which allows you to slide the blade into hard to reach places without damaging the flesh. For a typical round fish, start by using the tip of the knife to cut around the head of the fish, through the meat all the way to the bones. Carefully draw the tip of the blade from the head to the tip of the fish, sitting it flush against the backbone. Using small, careful incisions, start to pry the fillet away from the backbone, working all the way down to the belly. Flip the fish over and repeat with the other fillet, this time working from the tail up toward the head. Finish by removing the fillets by cutting through the skin of the detached fillets at the bottom. Grip the tail end of a fillet carefully between your fingers in one hand and remove the skin by holding the knife parallel to your chopping board, sliding it carefully between where the skin meets the flesh. Using a gently sawing motion, separate the fillet from the skin and trim before preparing and cooking.

For flatfish, such as Dover sole, bring a small saucepan of water to the boil. Dip the very end of the tail of the fish in the water for 5 seconds – this will make the skin easier to peel away. Hold the fish flat, topside facing up on a chopping board, and use a small paring knife to scrape the skin away from the tailbone. Use your fingers to pry the skin away from the tailbone until you can grip enough of it. Once you have enough skin in your grip you can start to pull the skin carefully, but steadily, away from the flesh. Flip the fish over and repeat for the bottom side. Now that you have skinned the fish, you can remove the fillets. Make sure the topside is facing up; you should see two fillets that meet at the middle of the backbone. Run the tip of your filleting knife in and under the top of one fillet at the head, and work it down to the tail, flush against the backbone, making small careful sweeps of the knife to separate the fillet from the bone. Cut the fillet away at the bottom before turning the fish around to remove the other fillet. Flip the fish over and repeat for the remaining two fillets. Discard any guts; the bones may be retained and cleaned in preparation for fish stock.

De-boning Fish

Now that you have separated the fillets from the fish, you may need to remove any bones that are attached to the flesh. Run your hands carefully over the flesh to see if you can detect any bones; some may be a little embedded in the fish so it is important to take care and time at this step. Using a pin-boner, or set of clean tweezers, pinch the end of the bone and pull carefully but firmly away and out of the flesh. The fillets can then be washed and dried before preparation and cooking.

Poaching Fish

Many fish dishes call for poaching the fish, either in a broth or in a sauce. Fish, such as haddock, can be poached in simmering milk, or fish stock until the flesh is firm with a slight spring to the touch. Fillets from flatfish, such as Dover sole, need to be scored lightly on their skin sides to prevent them from curling up and tightening during poaching. Poaching is an ideal way to cook fish gently and evenly, thus preventing it from overcooking and drying out.

Steaming Fish

Much like with poaching, steaming is a quick and convenient way to cook fish without fear of overcooking. Steaming tends to be a popular method of cooking in pan-Asian cuisine and is ideal for those seeking a healthier way to cook. After you have filleted your fish, line a steamer with a sheet of greaseproof paper. Lay the fillets of fish on the paper and drizzle with a little oil before seasoning. Cover the steamer with a lid and place over a saucepan of simmering water, until the fish is cooked through. Drain the fish on kitchen paper before serving.

Frying Fish

Frying fish is a fast and simple way of cooking. You can also fry fish with, or without the skin on for convenience. Make sure your fish has been prepared according to the recipe, removing any pin bones, if necessary. Heat a large frying, or sauté pan over a moderate heat until hot before adding a couple of tablespoons of oil to the pan; it is better to add a little more oil if in doubt to help prevent the fish from sticking to the pan. Season your fish fillets and place in the pan, skin-side down, making sure to not overcrowd the pan. A good practice when frying fish is to leave the fillets untouched initially; once the flesh on top is starting to turn opaque, carefully slide a fish slice underneath your fillets before flipping. Cook the other sides for 1-2 minutes until the flesh is firm yet springy to the touch; you can add a knob of butter to the pan at this point to help baste the fish, if desired. Remove from the pan and serve as soon as possible for best results.

Deep-frying Fish

Sometimes, there's nothing better than a piece of deep-fried cod to go with some thick-cut chips and mushy peas. As fish cooks so quickly, it needs to be battered before deep-frying to help prevent it from drying out. Firm, white-fleshed fish, such as cod, hake and haddock, are particularly good when deep-fried. Before deep-frying your fish, you will need to heat a good quantity of oil, such as vegetable oil, in a deep fryer, or heavy-based saucepan to 180°C / 350F. Prepare a quick batter by whisking together 300 g / 10 ½ oz / 2 cups self-raising flour with enough sparkling water until the batter is of a thick coating consistency. Trim and prepare your fillets of fish before dusting lightly in plain flour and a little seasoning; shake off the excess and arrange on a lined tray. Dip your fish in the batter to coat before dropping into the hot oil. Deep-fry for 3-4 minutes until golden brown all over; remove carefully from the hot oil and drain on kitchen paper before serving. Always remember to handle hot oil with caution.

Grilling Fish

For a healthier alternative to frying, or deep-frying fish, grilling is a great way to cook your fish in a light, nutritious manner. Fish, such as sea bass, Dover sole and bream, are ideal for grilling. Make sure that your grill is preheated to a moderately high heat. Place your fillets of fish on a grilling tray, skin side down, before rubbing with olive, or sunflower oil. Season with salt and pepper, as well as any other herbs and spices you would like. Place under the hot grill and leave the fish to cook until the flesh is slightly opaque and firm, yet springy to the touch; thicker fillets will take longer to cook. Remove from the grill and serve with a mixed salad, or green lentils for a quick, healthy supper.

Roasting Fish

When it comes to cooking larger pieces of fish, such as monkfish, or indeed whole fish, such as John Dory, roasting can be an effective and simple method. Start by preheating your oven to 190°C (170°C fan) / 375F / gas 5. Once your fish has been cleaned, descaled and gutted, make a few incisions in the skin, on both sides, with a sharp knife. Season the insides and outsides with salt and pepper and drizzle with olive, or sunflower oil. You could also stuff the whole fish with herbs, or slices of citrus fruit for example. Place the fish on an elevated trivet, sat in a roasting tin large enough to contain the fish. By elevating the fish, you will ensure an even circulation of heat around the fish as it roasts. Roast until the flesh is crisp and the flesh is firm with a very slight spring to the touch. As a guideline, for a 1.35 kg / 3 lb sea bass, it will need 25–30 minutes in the oven. Remove the fish from the oven and let it sit for a few minutes before serving.

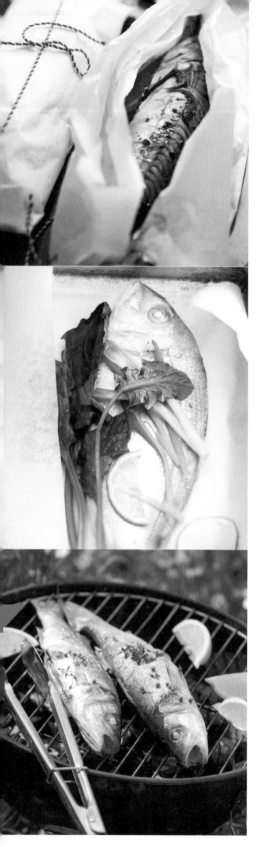

Wrapping Fish

A useful technique to know when cooking fish is cooking with the use of a parcel, or wrapper. This method is known as 'en papillote' and is used to help fish retain moisture as it bakes and steams in the oven. Preheat the oven to 180°C (160°C fan) / 350F / gas 4 and cut a square sheet of greaseproof paper, large enough to envelop a fillet of fish comfortably. Place the fish on the sheet of paper, drizzle with olive oil and season before bringing the sides up and over the fillet, scrunching them together to seal in a parcel. Place on a baking tray and bake until firm, yet slightly springy to the touch; take care when opening the parcel as the hot steam will escape quickly.

Barbecuing Fish

When the sun is out, barbecuing fish can be a delicious way to cook whole fish without the need to skin and fillet. Smaller fish, such as mackerel, are ideal for barbecues as they are easy to portion out, as well as being easy to flip. Clean, scale and gut the fish, then make a few slashes on both sides of the skin. Rub with olive oil and stuff with seasonings, such as chopped herbs. Place directly onto a hot grill that has been lightly oiled and cook on both sides until the skin is crisp and the flesh is cooked through. Larger round fish, such as bream or sea bass, also take well to being barbecued; adjust cooking times according to the size of fish.

SERVES: **4**

PREPARATION TIME: **20 MINUTES**

COOKING TIME: **30–40 MINUTES**

INGREDIENTS

110 g / 4 oz / ½ cup unsalted butter,
  softened
1 orange
a small handful of chive stalks
1 kg / 2 lb 4 oz / 6 ⅔ cups floury potatoes,
  peeled and evenly diced
110 ml / 4 fl. oz / ½ cup coconut milk
4 large turbot fillets, skinned, pin-boned
  and halved
salt and freshly ground black pepper

Orange Turbot with Coconut Mash

1. Preheat the oven to 200°C (180°C fan) / 400F / gas 6 and line a rimmed baking tray, or large roasting tin with greaseproof paper.

2. Juice and zest the orange. Combine half of the juice and zest with the butter and beat until smooth before covering and setting to one side.

3. Finely chop most of the chives and cut the rest in half, then set to one side.

4. Cook the potatoes in a large saucepan of salted, boiling water for 15–20 minutes until tender. Drain and leave to steam dry for a few minutes before mashing with the coconut milk and a little salt.

5. Arrange the turbot fillets on the baking tray and dot with the orange butter.

6. Bake for 16–20 minutes until the flesh is firm with a slight spring to the touch.

7. Remove from the oven and leave to rest for a few minutes as you reheat the mash.

8. Spoon the mash onto the middle of 4 serving plates before topping with the turbot fillets.

9. Spoon over the orange butter from the baking tray before garnishing with chives and the remaining orange juice and zest on top.

SERVES: **4**

PREPARATION TIME: **5–10 MINUTES**

COOKING TIME: **8–10 MINUTES**

INGREDIENTS

4 x 200 g / 7 oz cod fillets, pin-boned and
   trimmed
1 tbsp sunflower oil
1 large carrot, peeled and julienned
½ green pepper, deseeded and thinly sliced
1 onion, finely sliced
½ courgette (zucchini), julienned
1 tbsp rice wine vinegar
salt and freshly ground black pepper

Steamed Cod with Sliced Vegetables

1. Line a large steamer with a
   sheet of greaseproof paper and
   arrange the cod fillets on it.

2. Season with a little salt and
   pepper, then sit on top of a
   saucepan of simmering water.

3. Cook until the fillets are firm
   with a very slight spring to
   the touch; 8–10 minutes.

4. Meanwhile, heat the sunflower
   oil in a large sauté pan set
   over a medium heat.

5. Add the vegetables and sauté for 2–3
   minutes, then cover with a lid and
   cook over a reduced heat until soft.

6. Adjust the seasoning to taste using
   rice wine vinegar, salt and pepper.

7. Drain the cod fillets on sheets
   of kitchen paper before
   placing on serving plates.

8. Top with the vegetables
   and serve immediately.

SERVES: **4**

PREPARATION TIME: **10 MINUTES**

COOKING TIME: **12–15 MINUTES**

INGREDIENTS

a small bunch of flat-leaf parsley
300 g / 10 ½ oz / 2 cups salt cod,
    soaked in cold water overnight
8 large eggs, beaten
1 red chilli (chili), deseeded and finely
    chopped
2 large egg whites
2 tbsp unsalted butter
2 tbsp sunflower oil
salt and freshly ground black pepper

Salt Cod Omelettes

1. Chop most of the parsley, retaining a little for a garnish.

2. Drain and rinse the salt cod under cold running water, then pat dry and flake into a bowl.

3. Add the beaten egg, chilli, parsley and seasoning, stirring well.

4. Lightly whisk the egg whites with a pinch of salt in a clean bowl, then fold into the eggs and cod.

5. Heat together 1 tbsp of the butter and oil in a large frying pan set over a medium heat until hot.

6. Place a couple of individual metal rings in the pan and add a quarter of the salt cod and egg mixture to the rings.

7. Let them set and cook for 2–3 minutes, then flip and cook the other sides for 2 minutes until golden.

8. Remove and add the remaining butter and oil to the pan before cooking the remaining omelettes.

9. Serve with a little parsley garnish on top.

SERVES: **4**

PREPARATION TIME: **30 MINUTES**

COOKING TIME: **40 MINUTES**

INGREDIENTS

a small bunch of tarragon, chopped
a small bunch of flat-leaf parsley, chopped
2 tbsp olive oil
225 g / 8 oz / 1 cup mayonnaise
750 g / 1 lb 10 oz / 5 cups floury potatoes,
    peeled and cut into chips
1 l / 1 pint 16 fl. oz / 4 cups sunflower oil, for
    deep-frying
4 x 200 g / 7 oz skinless fillets of pollock, or
    haddock, pin-boned
55 g / 2 oz / ⅓ cup plain (all purpose) flour
2 large eggs, beaten
225 g / 8 oz / 2 cups golden breadcrumbs
2 lemons, halved
salt and freshly ground black pepper

Fish, Chips and Herb Mayonnaise

1. Blitz together the chopped herbs
   and oil with a little seasoning in a
   food processor until smooth.

2. Add the mayonnaise and blitz again
   until smooth. Adjust seasoning
   to taste, then cover and chill.

3. Cook the chipped potatoes in a large
   saucepan of salted, boiling water
   for 10–12 minutes until tender.

4. Drain and leave to cool
   for 10 minutes.

5. Heat the sunflower oil in a large,
   heavy-based saucepan, or deep-
   fat fryer to 160°C / 320F.

6. Fry the chips for 8–10 minutes until
   golden-brown and crisp. Drain and
   season, keeping warm to one side.

7. Season the fish before dusting in
   flour, shaking off any excess.

8. Dip in the egg and coat in
   breadcrumbs, then deep-fry
   for 4–5 minutes until golden.

9. Drain and serve alongside the chips,
   herb mayonnaise and lemon halves.

SERVES: **4**

PREPARATION TIME: **20–25 MINUTES**

COOKING TIME: **8–10 MINUTES**

INGREDIENTS

550 ml / 1 pint / 2 ¼ cups light vegetable
    stock
250 ml / 9 fl. oz / 1 cup light coconut milk
400 g / 14 oz / 2 cups orange lentils
8 x 150–175 g / 5–6 oz skinless fillets of
    salmon, trimmed
150 g / 5 oz / 1 ½ cups grated mozzarella
100 g / 3 ½ oz / 2 cups baby spinach
2 tbsp olive oil
2 plum tomatoes, diced
salt and freshly ground black pepper

Salmon, Spinach and Lentils

1. Combine the stock and coconut milk in a large saucepan, then boil and simmer.

2. Add the lentils, stir once, and cook at a simmer for 20–25 minutes until tender.

3. Meanwhile, preheat the oven to 220°C (200°C fan) / 425F / gas 7 and line a baking tray with greaseproof paper.

4. Top half of the salmon fillets with mozzarella and some of the spinach leaves.

5. Sit another salmon fillet on top and drizzle with olive oil before seasoning; transfer to the baking tray.

6. Roast for 8–10 minutes until the fish is firm with a very slight spring to the touch.

7. Drain the lentils, then stir through the tomatoes and adjust the seasoning to taste.

8. Spoon onto plates and sit the stuffed salmon on top.

9. Garnish with the remaining spinach leaves before serving.

SERVES: **4**

PREPARATION TIME: **15 MINUTES**

COOKING TIME: **12–14 MINUTES**

INGREDIENTS

55 ml / 2 fl. oz / ¼ cup olive oil
1 lemon, juiced
2 cloves of garlic, crushed
a small bunch of basil, chopped
75 g / 3 oz / ½ cup pitted black olives,
    chopped
4 x 200 g / 7 oz skinless salmon fillets,
    pin-boned
2 salad tomatoes, sliced
150 g / 5 oz / 1 cup buffalo mozzarella,
    cut into slices
400 g / 14 oz / 4 cups steamed rice, to
    serve
a large handful of rocket (arugula), to
    serve
salt and freshly ground black pepper

Salmon and Mozzarella Bake

1. Preheat the oven to 190°C (170°C fan) / 375F / gas 5.

2. Stir together the olive oil, lemon juice, garlic, basil and olives in a mixing bowl.

3. Sit the salmon fillets on sheets of foil, then alternate overlapping slices of tomato and mozzarella on top.

4. Spoon over the olive oil mixture and season generously.

5. Bring the foil over and around the salmon to envelop, sealing the edges together.

6. Arrange on a baking tray and bake for 12–14 minutes until the salmon is lightly opaque.

7. Open carefully before serving with the rice and rocket leaves.

SERVES: **4**

PREPARATION TIME: **10 MINUTES**

COOKING TIME: **6–10 MINUTES**

INGREDIENTS

4 x 300 g / 10 ½ oz tuna steaks
2 tbsp sunflower oil
2 green peppers, deseeded and finely
 diced
2 red peppers, deseeded and finely
 diced
a small handful of rocket (arugula), to
 garnish
salt and freshly ground black pepper

Grilled Tuna Steak

1. Preheat the grill, or barbecue to hot.

2. Brush the tuna steaks with sunflower
 oil and season generously.

3. Grill for 3–5 minutes on
 both sides, depending on
 desired cooking degree.

4. Serve on a bed of diced peppers,
 garnished with rocket leaves.

SERVES: **6–8**

PREPARATION TIME: **20–25 MINUTES**

COOKING TIME: **50–60 MINUTES**

INGREDIENTS

750 g / 1 lb 10 oz / 5 cups skinless salmon
    fillet, diced
1 bay leaf
a few black peppercorns
350 g / 12 oz ready-made shortcrust pastry
a little plain (all purpose) flour, for dusting
5–6 cooked ham slices
100 g / 3 ½ oz / 2 cups Swiss chard
225 g / 8 oz / 2 cups steamed basmati rice
1 large egg, beaten
salt and freshly ground black pepper

Salmon Pie

1. Preheat the oven to 160°C (140°C fan) / 325F / gas 3.

2. Place the salmon, peppercorns and bay leaf in a saucepan and cover with just enough water to submerge the fish. Bring to a simmer over a medium heat and poach for 5–6 minutes until just cooked.

3. Remove from the heat and strain the salmon, discarding the bay leaf and peppercorns as you do.

4. Flake the fish in a bowl and leave to cool. Roll out two-thirds of the pastry on a floured surface and use to line the base and sides of an 18 cm (7 in) springform cake tin.

5. Line the base of the pastry with slices of the ham. Top with half of the flaked salmon, then cover with a thin layer of chard.

6. Top with the rice and smooth down, then top with more chard and the remaining salmon on top. Roll out the remaining pastry into a 20 cm (8 in) round, approximately ¾ cm (¼ in) thick.

7. Sit on top of the salmon, tucking in the edges against the pastry on the sides. Brush the top with the beaten egg and bake for 50–60 minutes until golden brown and cooked.

8. Remove to a wire rack to cool before turning out and slicing.

Preparing Shellfish

With shellfish, it is really important to buy your produce as fresh as possible; the fresher the better. Shellfish that is a few days old will have a distinctly fishy smell, as well as taking longer to cook and being potentially harmful. Where possible, try and buy mussels, prawns and scallops from your fishmonger on the day they have been caught. To prepare scallops, an oyster knife is useful to open the shells; if not, a sharp, flexible filleting knife will work adequately. Carefully slide your knife between the shells, gradually twisting it and working upwards to pry the shells open. Remove any dark organs attached to the white muscle meat and the roe (if attached). You can use the roe in some instances, although for most it is best to discard. Carefully rinse the muscle meat and pat dry before cooking.

For mussels, rinse them in cold, running water before pulling away any beards that are attached using your fingers; they may need some force to be removed. Pinch together the shells of any opened mussels; if they do not close, discard them. The mussels are now ready to be cooked.

When dealing with prawns, you may want to leave them intact for presentation purposes. If not, twist off the head and discard. Peel the shell around the body and tail; discard. Use a small paring knife to make a thin incision down the spine of the prawn. Pick out the stringy intestine along with any grit. Gently wash the prawns and pat dry before cooking. Even when cooking prawns with the shell on, it is best to remove the intestine before eating.

Cooking Mussels

When cooking mussels, the best approach is to steam them open. Set a large saucepan, or casserole dish over a moderate heat until hot. Add a little butter and leave to melt before sweating some onion, or shallot with a little garlic. Add your mussels as well as a small glass of white wine, or cider. Bring the liquid to a simmer before covering with a lid and leaving to cook for 3–5 minutes until the shells have opened; discard any that haven't opened after steaming. They can be enjoyed simply as is with some crusty bread, or you could add a dash of cream for a more luxurious dish.

Cooking Prawns

Prawns are ideally suited to fast cooking methods, such as pan-frying, grilling, or barbecuing. To cook them on the barbecue, make sure the coals are white hot for a coal barbecue, or that you have set a gas barbecue to a moderately high temperature. Thread your prawns onto skewers; if they are wooden, make sure you have soaked them in water for 30 minutes beforehand to prevent burning. Brush the prawns with olive oil and season lightly before grilling for 4–5 minutes, turning once, until pink and firm yet springy to the touch. Serve with wedges of lemon to squeeze over.

Cooking Scallops

Scallops also cook very quickly; an overcooked scallop is quite unappetising, so it is important to always be present when cooking them. For eight scallops, heat a large frying or sauté pan over a moderate heat until hot. Add 1 ½ tbsp sunflower oil and season your scallops on both sides before placing in the pan in a circle; try and work quickly so as to keep cooking times even. Flip the scallops after 60–90 seconds once the undersides are golden brown. Cook the other sides for a further 60–90 seconds depending on size until golden brown; they should be firm yet springy to the touch. Scallops go particularly well with fresh herbs and cured pork meat, such as bacon or pancetta.

Crab and Lobster

Extracting meat from crab, or lobster claws and shells is an involved process. Here are a few tips to help you out when you want to get as much meat from them as possible. Make sure you have a lobster, or nutcracker to hand, as well as a lobster, or crab pick. Using the cracker, crack the shell of the claws firmly, peeling away pieces of shell with your fingers. Use the pick to scoop out meat from the ends, or in nooks. For lobster tails, you should be able to separate the tail from the body in one piece using your hands. From there you can lightly crack the shell, then peel it away. If you are serving lobster and crab legs at the table, diners can simply crack them before sucking out the meat. Once you have extracted as much meat as possible, sift through the flesh to check for pieces of shell before serving.

Squid and Octopus

Squid and octopus can be tricky to source fresh, but they are at their best when fresh rather than frozen. Preparing squid and octopus can seem daunting initially, but with practice it becomes easy. For squid, pull the tentacles away from the body. Inside the body will be the quill – it will feel like a plastic feather – remove it and discard. Pull the ears off the body and remove the purple skin from both the ears and body. Cut the tentacles off just below the eyes of the squid; towards the middle of the tentacles will be a hard beak which you should discard. Pull out any guts and discard, but watch out for the ink sack, which can be used to when making risotto, or pasta dough. The main body can be either stuffed, or cut into rings. If you do cut the body into rings, score the insides with a sharp knife to prevent excess curling during cooking.

For octopus, you need to remove the small middle section between the head and tentacles. Cut through that part just above the tentacles (below the eyes) and just at the bottom of the head section. Turn the tentacles over and locate the beak before discarding. Turn the head inside out and pull out the insides. Wash the tentacles and head clean of any ink, rinsing thoroughly in any holes or suckers. Pat dry and pull the skin off the head section; you can trim the base for a tidier finish at this point.

Squid and octopus cook quickly, which makes them susceptible to overcooking. In order to tenderise them as much possible, lightly pound with a meat hammer before cooking, especially when cooking octopus. Pan-frying is usually the simplest method for cooking this type of seafood, although both are delicious either braised for maximum tenderness, or cooked on a barbecue, or on a griddle in Mediterranean style.

SERVES: **4**

PREPARATION TIME: **20 MINUTES**

COOKING TIME: **15–20 MINUTES**

INGREDIENTS

4 chive stalks
300 g / 10 ½ oz / 2 cups mussels,
  cleaned with beards removed
150 ml / 5 fl. oz / ⅔ cup dry white wine
1 small head of broccoli, prepared into
  small florets
200 g / 7 oz / 1 ⅓ cups frozen baby
  prawns (shrimp), thawed
75 ml / 3 fl. oz / ⅓ cup double (heavy)
  cream
a small bunch of flat-leaf parsley,
  chopped
1 large sheet of ready-made filo pastry,
  kept under a damp towel
½ tsp curry powder, to garnish
salt and freshly ground black pepper

Seafood and Broccoli Pastry Purses

1. Preheat the oven to 200°C (180°C fan) / 400F / gas 6; line a baking tray with greaseproof paper.

2. Blanch the chive stalks in a bowl of boiling water for 5 seconds before removing.

3. Heat a large saucepan over a moderate heat until hot before adding the mussels and wine.

4. Cover with a lid and allow the steam to cook the mussels for 4–5 minutes until opened.

5. Drain the mussels and discard any that haven't opened.

6. Remove the meat from the shells and return to the pan before adding the broccoli florets, prawns, cream and parsley.

7. Cook over a medium heat for 2 minutes before seasoning.

8. Cut the sheet of pastry into 4 even squares; spoon the filling onto the middle of the squares using a slotted spoon.

9. Bring the edges of the pastry up and around the filling, gathering them in a knot above and tying using the blanched chive stalks.

10. Place on the baking tray and bake for 15–20 minutes until the pastry is golden brown and cooked.

11. Remove from the oven and leave to cool for a few minutes before garnishing with a pinch of curry powder.

SERVES: **4**

PREPARATION TIME: **30–40 MINUTES**

COOKING TIME: **10 MINUTES**

INGREDIENTS

1 tbsp unsalted butter
450 g / 1 lb / 3 cups mussels, cleaned with
   beards removed
175 ml / 6 fl. oz / ¾ cup dry white wine
2 fennel bulbs, thinly sliced
2 tbsp olive oil
1 lemon, juiced
a small bunch of chervil, chopped
salt and freshly ground black pepper

Mussel and Fennel Salad

1. Melt the butter in a large saucepan set over a moderate heat.

2. Add the mussels and cook for 1 minute, stirring occasionally, before adding the wine.

3. Cover with a lid and allow the steam to cook the mussels for 3–4 minutes until opened.

4. Drain the mussels and discard any that haven't opened.

5. Remove the mussel meat from the shells and place in a bowl, leaving to cool for 5 minutes; cover and chill until cold.

6. Once chilled, toss the mussel meat with the sliced fennel, olive oil, lemon juice, half of the chervil and some seasoning.

7. Spoon into serving dishes and serve with the remaining chervil sprinkled over.

SERVES: **4**

PREPARATION TIME: **25 MINUTES**

COOKING TIME: **NONE**

INGREDIENTS

a small bunch of chive stalks
2 lemons, juiced
1 lime, juiced
75 ml / 3 fl. oz / ⅓ cup extra-virgin
    olive oil
300 g / 10 ½ oz / 2 cups white crab
    meat, picked
4 kiwis, peeled and diced
salt and freshly ground black pepper

Crab and Kiwi Citrus Salad

1. Finely chop half of the chives,
   keeping the remainder whole.

2. Mix together the chopped chives,
   lemon juice, lime juice, olive oil and a
   little seasoning in a large mixing bowl.

3. Add the crab meat; stir, cover
   and chill for at least 15 minutes.

4. Stir through the kiwi fruit
   before spooning the mixture
   into serving glasses.

5. Garnish with a little extra pepper
   and chive stalks before serving.

SERVES: **4**

PREPARATION TIME: **10 MINUTES**

COOKING TIME: **10 MINUTES**

INGREDIENTS

300 g / 10 ½ oz / 3 cups spaghetti
12 queen scallops, roe removed
2 tbsp sunflower oil
1 tbsp olive oil
1 red pepper, deseeded and finely diced
1 yellow pepper, deseeded and finely
   diced
1 medium courgette (zucchini), finely
   diced
½ large aubergine (eggplant), finely
   diced
1 large clove of garlic, minced
½ tsp dried thyme
½ tsp dried oregano
salt and freshly ground black pepper

Spaghetti with Scallops

1. Cook the spaghetti in a large saucepan of salted, boiling water until 'al dente'; 8–10 minutes approximately.

2. Season the scallops and heat a large sauté pan over a moderate heat until hot.

3. Add the sunflower oil and sear the scallops for 1 minute on each side; remove from the pan.

4. Add the olive oil to the pan before adding the peppers, courgette and aubergine.

5. Sauté with a little seasoning for 2–3 minutes before adding the garlic and dried herbs.

6. Cook for a further minute before reducing the heat a little and returning the scallops to pan.

7. Reserve ½ cup of the cooking liquid before draining the pasta and adding to the pan.

8. Toss well, adding a little of the cooking liquid to loosen if necessary.

9. Adjust the seasoning to taste before serving.

SERVES: **4**

PREPARATION TIME: **20 MINUTES**

COOKING TIME: **4–6 MINUTES**

INGREDIENTS

a small bunch of flat-leaf parsley
2 lemons
75 ml / 3 fl. oz / ⅓ cup olive oil
½ red chilli (chili), deseeded and
    chopped
2 cloves of garlic, minced
1 tsp smoked paprika
a pinch of caster (superfine) sugar
350 g / 12 oz / 2 ⅓ cups diced, skinless
    salmon fillet
300 g / 10 ½ oz / 2 cups prawns
    (shrimp), peeled and deveined
12 queen scallops, roe removed
12 wooden skewers, soaked in water
    for 30 minutes beforehand
salt and freshly ground black pepper

Seafood Tapas on Sticks

1. Finely chop most of the parsley and combine with the juice of one lemon in a mixing bowl; cut the other lemon into wedges.

2. Add the oil, chilli, garlic, paprika, sugar, and some seasoning to the mixing bowl.

3. Add the salmon, prawns and scallops and mix well; cover and chill for 15 minutes.

4. Preheat the grill, or a barbecue to a moderately hot temperature.

5. Thread a combination of the seafood and fish onto the skewers and arrange on a tray.

6. Grill for 2–3 minutes on each side until lightly charred and cooked through; they should feel firm with a very slight spring to the touch.

7. Remove from the grill and serve with lemon wedges and extra parsley as a garnish.

SERVES: **4**

PREPARATION TIME: **5 MINUTES**

COOKING TIME: **4–5 MINUTES**

INGREDIENTS

12 queen scallops, roe removed
2 tbsp sunflower oil
1 tbsp truffle oil
1 large carrot, peeled and cut into thin
   batons
1 green pepper, deseeded and thinly
   sliced
1 yellow pepper, deseeded and thinly
   sliced
salt and freshly ground black pepper

Roasted Scallops with Truffle Oil

1. Preheat the oven to 200°C
   (180°C fan) / 400F / gas 6.

2. Coat the scallops in the sunflower
   oil and half of the truffle oil
   before seasoning generously.

3. Arrange in a circle in an ovenproof
   pan; roast for 4–5 minutes until
   golden on both sides, flipping them
   if necessary halfway through.

4. Remove from the oven and transfer
   to serving plates with a slotted spoon.

5. Serve with the vegetables
   and a little drizzle of the
   remaining truffle oil on top.

VEGETABLES

Types of Vegetables

Vegetables are a versatile produce, coming in a variety of shapes and sizes, and with various uses in cooking. Whether they are starchy, such as potatoes and pumpkins, or light and fresh like an iceberg lettuce, or cucumber, vegetables are an important part of many cuisines and recipes. They often provide the perfect foil to meats and fish, and are generally speaking, easy to prepare. Vegetables are also a cheap and important source of vitamins and nutrients; meeting the recommended dietary requirement of 'five a day' is made easier with a selection of delicious vegetarian recipes to prepare at home.

Vegetables can be subdivided into various categories. Leafy vegetables tend to be rich in Vitamin B9, as well as providing a good source of iron and appearing dark green in colour – spinach is a good example of such a vegetable. Most beans can be classed as pod vegetables; green, runner and mangetout are all in this family, among others. Courgettes and aubergines are fruit vegetables and are a great source of fibre and Vitamin C. Carrots, parsnips and turnips all fall under the branch of root vegetables and are low in calories, with some varieties containing high levels of Vitamin A. Brassicas, such as cauliflower and broccoli and vegetables such as asparagus, are examples of flower and bud vegetables.

Cooking times for vegetables vary greatly; a handful of spinach will wilt in less than a minute when added to hot oil or butter. Potatoes, however, ideally need to be cooked in boiling water until they become tender. Some vegetables, such as carrots and asparagus, can be eaten both cooked and raw. Eating vegetables raw provides the highest level of nutrients and minerals; when vegetables are cooked, they lose some of their natural goodness. As such, a simple salad is a great way to maximise as many nutrients and minerals when using vegetables. Always remember to wash vegetables really well before preparing.

Boiling Vegetables

For root vegetables, such as turnip and swede, peel and dice into even chunks. Cook in a large saucepan of salted, boiling water for 15–20 minutes until tender. Drain and leave to steam dry for a few minutes before preparing. For green vegetables, such as mange tout, green beans and asparagus, cook for only 2–3 minutes, depending on volume of vegetables. These kinds of vegetables should still have a little crunch to them once cooked. To help them retain their crunch, they can be plunged immediately into a large bowl of iced water to stop the cooking process. Drain and dry off before using in your recipe, or serving as an accompaniment.

Roasting Vegetables

Vegetables, such as carrots and parsnips, benefit from roasting to bring out their natural sweetness, as do white, yellow and red onions. Preheat your oven to 190°C (170°C fan) / 375F / gas 5 before peeling and cutting your vegetables into even batons, or chunks. Toss the cut vegetables in a little oil before seasoning and arranging in roasting tins, or on baking trays. Roast for 40–50 minutes until golden brown at the edges and tender within. Serve with roasted meats, or fish for a simple supper.

Steaming Vegetables

Vegetables that cook quickly, such as mange tout and green beans, are perfect for steaming. Steaming has the added benefit of helping vegetables to retain as many nutrients as possible during the cooking process. Place your vegetables in a steamer before sitting over a saucepan of gently simmering water. Cover with a lid and allow the steam to cook the vegetables until tender. Drain on kitchen paper, if necessary, before serving.

Grilling and Frying

Some firmer types of vegetable need to be blanched in hot water before grilling, or frying. For example, to grill carrots or asparagus, blanch in a saucepan of salted, boiling water for 1 minute before draining and patting dry. Drizzle with oil and season with salt and pepper before grilling for 4–5 minutes, turning occasionally. For frying, lightly coat a frying pan with oil and place over a moderate heat until hot. Season your vegetables before pan-frying for 3–4 minutes.

SERVES: **4**

PREPARATION TIME: **10 MINUTES**

COOKING TIME: **15 MINUTES**

INGREDIENTS

1 head of Savoy cabbage, outer layers
  removed
1 tbsp sunflower oil
150 g / 5 oz / 1 cup bacon lardons
1 tbsp unsalted butter
150 ml / 5 fl. oz / ⅔ cup double (heavy)
  cream
salt and freshly ground black pepper

Cabbage and Bacon Stir-fry

1. Shred the cabbage using a
   sharp knife; set to one side.

2. Heat the oil in a large casserole dish,
   or saucepan set over a medium heat.

3. Add the lardons and sauté
   for 3–4 minutes, stirring
   occasionally, until golden.

4. Remove the lardons from the dish
   and drain on kitchen paper.

5. Add the butter to the dish and
   let it melt before adding the
   cabbage and a little seasoning.

6. Cook over a medium heat for
   4–5 minutes, stirring occasionally,
   until it starts to soften.

7. Return the bacon to the dish and
   add the cream; cook for a further
   2–3 minutes before adjusting the
   seasoning to taste; serve warm.

SERVES: **4**

PREPARATION TIME: **30 MINUTES**

COOKING TIME: **20–25 MINUTES**

INGREDIENTS

2 small heads of cauliflower, prepared
   into florets
2 tbsp unsalted butter
2 tbsp plain (all purpose) flour
600 ml / 1 pint 2 fl. oz / 2 ½ cups whole
   milk
a pinch of grated nutmeg
150 g / 5 oz / 1 ½ cups Cheddar, grated
salt and pepper

Cauliflower Gratin

1. Preheat the oven to 190°C
   (170°C fan) / 375F / gas 5.

2. Cook the cauliflower in a large
   saucepan of salted, boiling water
   for 6–8 minutes, until just tender.

3. Drain well and leave to steam dry.

4. Meanwhile, melt the butter in a
   saucepan set over a moderate heat.

5. Whisk in the flour to make a roux,
   cooking until golden in appearance.

6. Whisk in the milk in a slow,
   steady stream until you
   have a thickened sauce.

7. Simmer over a reduced heat for
   4–5 minutes, stirring occasionally,
   before whisking in the nutmeg
   and 100 g of the Cheddar.

8. Cook for a further 2 minutes before
   adjusting the seasoning to taste.

9. Arrange the cauliflower in a
   baking dish before pouring
   over the cheese sauce.

10. Sprinkle over the remaining
    Cheddar before baking for 20–25
    minutes until golden on top.

11. Remove from the oven
    and leave to stand for a few
    minutes before serving.

INGREDIENTS

750 g / 1 lb 10 oz / 5 cups waxy potatoes
1 large head of broccoli, prepared into
    florets
2 tbsp unsalted butter
2 tbsp plain (all purpose) flour
600 ml / 1 pint 2 fl. oz / 2 ½ cups whole milk
110 g / 4 oz / 1 cup Roquefort, or
    Gorgonzola, cubed
salt and pepper

Broccoli and Potato Gratin

1. Cook the potatoes in a large saucepan of salted, boiling water for 15–20 minutes until tender; remove with a slotted spoon and leave to steam dry to one side.

2. Add the broccoli to the water and cook for 3–4 minutes until tender; drain and leave on one side to dry.

3. Preheat the oven to 190°C (170°C fan) / 375F / gas 5.

4. Melt the butter in a saucepan set over a moderate heat; whisk in the flour and cook until a roux forms.

5. Cook until golden in appearance before whisking in the milk in a slow, steady stream until a sauce forms.

6. Simmer over a reduced heat for 4–5 minutes until thickened; adjust seasoning to taste.

7. Pour the sauce into a baking dish before arranging the potatoes and broccoli in it.

8. Dot cubes of blue cheese on top and bake for 20–25 minutes.

9. Remove from the oven and leave to stand for a few minutes before serving.

SERVES: **4**

PREPARATION TIME: **10 MINUTES**

COOKING TIME: **15–20 MINUTES**

INGREDIENTS

600 g / 1 lb 5 oz / 4 cups turnips,
    peeled and diced
600 g / 1 lb 5 oz / 4 cups floury
    potatoes, peeled and diced
2 tbsp sunflower oil
½ tsp cumin seeds
2 tsp ground coriander (cilantro)
1 tsp ground cumin
2 tsp Madras curry powder
a pinch of caster (superfine) sugar
150 g / 5 oz / 3 cups baby spinach,
    washed
salt and freshly ground black pepper

Curried Turnips, Potatoes and Spinach

1. Cook the turnips and potatoes in separate saucepans of salted, boiling water for 15–20 minutes, until they are tender.

2. Drain them both and leave to steam dry to one side.

3. Heat the sunflower oil in a large casserole dish, or saucepan set over a medium heat.

4. Add the cumin seeds, fry for 15–20 seconds until fragrant before adding the ground spices and sugar.

5. Stir-fry for a further 20–30 seconds before adding the cooked turnip and potato.

6. Stir well to coat and cook for 3–4 minutes until lightly browned; add the spinach and cook until wilted.

7. Adjust the seasoning to taste before spooning into dishes and serving.

INGREDIENTS

150 g / 5 oz / ⅔ cup unsalted butter,
  softened
2 cloves of garlic, minced
a small bunch of flat-leaf parsley, finely
  chopped
4 medium corn on the cob
2 tbsp sunflower oil
salt and freshly ground black pepper

Grilled Corn on the Cob

1. Beat together the butter, garlic and parsley with a little seasoning in a small mixing bowl until combined.

2. Spoon onto a piece of cling film and roll into a rough sausage shape before chilling until firm; 30–40 minutes.

3. Meanwhile, preheat a grill, or barbecue to hot and place the corn in a bowl of cold water to soak for 15 minutes; drain and pat dry.

4. Brush the corn with a little sunflower oil and season generously.

5. Cook under the grill, or on a barbecue for 12–15 minutes, turning occasionally, until lightly charred all over.

6. Serve immediately with the prepared butter on the side.

INGREDIENTS

110 ml / 4 fl. oz / ½ cup sunflower oil
4 medium, or large parsnips, peeled
2 large red onions
½ small pumpkin
750 g / 1 lb 10 oz / 5 cups Charlotte potatoes
2 tsp dried thyme
2 tsp dried rosemary
2 tsp caster (superfine) sugar

Old-fashioned, Roasted Vegetables

1. Preheat the oven to 190°C (170°C fan) / 375F / gas 5.

2. Split the parsnips in half and cut the red onions into large chunks.

3. Wash and dry the potatoes, cutting any larger ones into smaller chunks so that they are all evenly sized.

4. Cut the pumpkin in half through the middle, and then remove any seeds and stringy pulp.

5. Turn the halves on their sides so that they are stable; cut into 2 cm (1 in) thick slices.

6. Divide the prepared vegetables between two shallow roasting tins.

7. Drizzle evenly with the sunflower oil and season each tray of vegetables with half the dried herbs, sugar and seasoning; toss well to coat.

8. Cover the trays loosely with foil and roast for 45 minutes; check to see if the vegetables are tender.

9. If they are, remove the foil, increase the oven to 220°C (200°C fan) / 425F / gas 7 and roast uncovered for a further 10–15 minutes.

10. If they need more time, return to the oven covered with the foil, checking every 5 minutes to see if they are tender.

11. Remove the vegetables after they have had 10–15 minutes in the oven, uncovered; serve immediately.

SERVES: **4**

PREPARATION TIME: **10–15 MINUTES**

COOKING TIME: **15 MINUTES**

INGREDIENTS

2 medium leeks
1 tbsp sunflower oil
2 tbsp unsalted butter
1 large onion, finely chopped
1 clove of garlic, minced
2 tbsp double (heavy) cream
75 g / 3 oz / ½ cup prosciutto, finely
   chopped
75 g / 3 oz / ¾ cup Parmesan, finely grated
salt and freshly ground black pepper

Chopped Leeks with Ham

1. Finely slice the leeks and wash in a colander under cold running water; drain and dry well.

2. Heat a large casserole dish over a medium heat before adding the oil and butter.

3. Add the onion, garlic and leek and sweat for 8–10 minutes, stirring occasionally, until softened.

4. Add the cream, stirring well, before cooking for a further 2–3 minutes; adjust the seasoning to taste.

5. Preheat the grill to hot.

6. Spoon the vegetables into heatproof serving bowls and top with the ham and Parmesan.

7. Flash under the grill for 1–2 minutes until the ham is lightly grilled.

8. Remove and leave to stand for a few minutes before serving.

SERVES: **4**

PREPARATION TIME: **10–15 MINUTES**

COOKING TIME: **3–4 MINUTES**

INGREDIENTS

1.25 l / 2 pints 4 fl. oz / 5 cups vegetable oil,
  for deep-frying
2 large onions
150 g / 5 oz / 1 cup cornflour (cornstarch)
175 ml / 6 fl. oz / ¾ cup sparkling water, cold
1 tsp salt
½ tsp paprika
½ tsp ground black pepper
½ tsp caster (superfine) sugar

Battered Onion Rings

1. Heat the oil in a large, heavy-based saucepan, or deep-fat fryer to 180°C (160°C fan) / 350F / gas 4.

2. Cut the onions horizontally into thick slices.

3. Whisk together the cornflour, sparkling water, salt, paprika, pepper and sugar to make a simple batter.

4. Dip the onion rings into the batter, letting the excess drip off before deep-frying for 3–4 minutes until golden and crisp.

5. Remove carefully and drain on paper towels before serving.

INGREDIENTS

2 tbsp olive oil
4 cloves of garlic, roughly chopped
2 spring onions (scallions), finely sliced
150 g / 5 oz / 1 ½ cups mange tout
150 g / 5 oz / 1 ½ cups French (string)
  beans
salt and freshly ground black pepper

Pan-fried Peas and French Beans

1. Heat the oil in a large sauté pan or wok set over a moderate heat.

2. Add the garlic and spring onions and sauté for 1 minute, stirring occasionally, before adding the mange tout and French beans.

3. Cover the dish with a lid and leave to cook for 2 minutes before removing the lid.

4. Continue to stir-fry for a further 2 minutes before adjusting the seasoning to taste.

5. Spoon into bowls and serve immediately.

SERVES: **4**

PREPARATION TIME: **35 MINUTES**

COOKING TIME: **4–6 MINUTES**

INGREDIENTS

225 g / 8 oz / 2 cups asparagus, woody
  ends removed
2 tbsp olive oil
4 small wooden skewers, soaked in
  cold water for 30 minutes
  beforehand
flaked sea salt and cracked black
  pepper

Grilled Green Asparagus

1. Preheat the grill or barbecue to hot.

2. Brush the asparagus spears with
   olive oil before threading four
   securely onto each skewer.

3. Season and grill for 4–6
   minutes, turning occasionally,
   until lightly charred.

4. Serve with extra flaked sea salt
   and cracked black pepper on top.

SERVES: **4**

PREPARATION TIME: **10 MINUTES**

COOKING TIME: **10–15 MINUTES**

INGREDIENTS

2 tbsp unsalted butter
½ onion, finely chopped
225 g / 8 oz / 2 cups frozen peas,
   thawed
a small handful of mint leaves, chopped
350 ml / 12 fl. oz / 1 ½ cups vegetable
   stock
75 ml / 3 fl. oz / ⅓ cup double (heavy)
   cream
a few sprigs of mint leaves, to garnish
salt and pepper

Cream of Pea and Mint Soup

1. Melt the butter in a large saucepan set over a medium heat.

2. Add the onion and sweat for 3–4 minutes until softened before adding 200 g of the peas and the chopped mint.

3. Continue to cook for 3–4 minutes, stirring occasionally.

4. Cover with the stock and cream and bring to a simmer.

5. Purée the soup until smooth in a food blender, or using a stick blender; adjust the seasoning to taste.

6. Reheat if necessary before ladling into soup bowls; garnish with the remaining peas and a sprig of mint leaves.

INGREDIENTS

450 g / 1 lb / 3 cups waxy potatoes, peeled
and cut into wedges
110 ml / 4 fl. oz / ½ cup olive oil
2 tbsp malt vinegar
a pinch of caster (superfine) sugar
½ tsp cumin seeds, toasted
a pinch of red chilli (chili) flakes
a small bunch of coriander (cilantro), roughly
chopped
225 g / 8 oz / 2 cups runner beans, roughly
chopped
225 g / 8 oz / 2 cups peeled broad (fava) beans
100 g / 3 ½ oz / ⅔ cup Kalamata olives
salt and freshly ground black pepper

Broad Bean and Runner Bean Salad

1. Cook the wedges of potato in a
   large saucepan of salted, boiling
   water for 12–15 minutes until tender;
   drain and leave to steam dry.

2. Whisk together the olive oil, vinegar,
   sugar, cumin seeds, and chilli flakes
   with most of the coriander and a
   little seasoning to make a dressing.

3. Blanch the runner beans and
   broad beans in a large saucepan
   of salted, boiling water for 2
   minutes; drain and refresh in iced
   water before draining well.

4. Arrange the beans, potatoes
   and olives on serving plates
   before dressing.

5. Garnish with the remaining
   coriander and serve.

SERVES: **4**

PREPARATION TIME: **15 MINUTES**

COOKING TIME: **25 MINUTES**

INGREDIENTS

600 g / 1 lb 5 oz / 4 cups baby turnips
2 tbsp sunflower oil
1 tbsp unsalted butter
a few chive stalks, chopped
a few sprigs of chervil
salt and freshly ground black pepper

Sautéed Baby Turnips

1. Trim the stalks of the baby turnips before cutting any larger ones in half so that the turnips are evenly sized.

2. Cook the turnips in a large saucepan of salted, boiling water for 12–15 minutes, until just tender.

3. Drain and leave to steam dry for a few minutes.

4. Heat the sunflower oil in a large sauté, or frying pan set over a moderate heat until hot.

5. Add the butter and let it foam before adding the turnips; sauté for 6–8 minutes, turning occasionally, until golden on the outside.

6. Chop a little chervil before sprinkling over the turnips along with the chives; adjust the seasoning to taste.

7. Spoon into a bowl and garnish with the remaining chervil before serving.

SERVES: **4**

PREPARATION TIME: **30–35 MINUTES**

COOKING TIME: **15–20 MINUTES**

INGREDIENTS

2 small heads of celeriac (celery root),
   peeled and diced evenly
1.2 l / 2 pint 4 fl. oz / 5 cups semi-skimmed
   milk
2 tbsp unsalted butter
75 g / 3 oz / ¾ cup Cheddar, grated
55 g / 2 oz / ½ cup Parmesan, grated
salt and pepper

Cheese-topped Celeriac Bake

1. Preheat the oven to 200°C
   (180°C fan) / 400F / gas 6.

2. Place the celeriac in a large
   saucepan and cover with the milk;
   bring to a simmer and cook for
   18–22 minutes, until tender.

3. Drain, reserving the cooking liquid,
   and leave to steam dry for a few
   minutes before mashing with
   butter and a little of the cooking
   liquid, if necessary, until smooth.

4. Adjust the seasoning to taste
   before dividing between four
   individual baking dishes.

5. Sprinkle the tops with the
   grated cheeses before
   arranging on a baking tray.

6. Bake for 15–20 minutes until
   golden and bubbling on top.

7. Remove from the oven and
   leave to stand for a few
   minutes before serving.

SERVES: **4**

PREPARATION TIME: **35 MINUTES**

COOKING TIME: **15–20 MINUTES**

INGREDIENTS

1 tbsp sunflower oil
2 tsp black sesame seeds
1 clove of garlic, crushed
150 g / 5 oz / 1 cup basmati rice, rinsed in
   several changes of cold water before
   draining
300 ml / 10 ½ fl. oz / 1 ½ cups hot water
a few strands of saffron, added to the hot
   water to infuse
4 red Espelette peppers
1 tbsp olive oil
a few chive stalks, chopped
salt

Peppers Stuffed with Saffron Rice

1. Heat the sunflower oil in a large saucepan set over a moderate heat.

2. Add the black sesame seeds and garlic and sauté for 30 seconds before adding the rice.

3. Stir well and cook for 1 minute before adding the infused hot water and 1 tsp of salt.

4. Stir once and bring the mixture to a simmer before covering with a lid and cooking over a reduced heat for 12–15 minutes, or until the rice has absorbed the liquid.

5. Remove from the heat and leave the rice covered as you prepare the peppers.

6. Preheat the oven to 190°C (170°C fan) / 375F / gas 5.

7. Run the tip of a sharp knife down one side of the peppers to open them up; remove any ribs and seeds and discard.

8. Fluff the rice with a fork before spooning into the peppers.

9. Arrange the stuffed peppers on a baking tray and drizzle with olive oil.

10. Bake for 15–20 minutes until the skin is starting to peel and the flesh is softened.

11. Remove from the oven and garnish with chives before serving.

INGREDIENTS

750 g / 1 lb 10 oz / 5 cups cooked
    beetroot in juice
2 tbsp sunflower oil
a small bunch of chives, chopped
salt and freshly ground black pepper

Roast Beetroot

1. Preheat the oven to 190°C
   (170°C fan) / 375F / gas 5.

2. Drain the beetroot and pat
   dry before cutting into evenly
   sized wedges or chunks.

3. Place in a roasting tin and
   drizzle over the oil; toss well
   to coat before seasoning.

4. Roast for 30–35 minutes
   until glistening.

5. Remove from the oven and garnish
   with chopped chives before serving.

SERVES: **4**

PREPARATION TIME: **10–15 MINUTES**

COOKING TIME: **18–20 MINUTES**

INGREDIENTS

150 g / 5 oz / 1 cup soft goats' cheese
75 g / 3 oz / ½ cup prosciutto, finely
  chopped
300 g / 10 ½ oz / 4 cups button mushrooms,
  stalks removed
2 tbsp olive oil
a few sprigs of coriander (cilantro), to
  garnish
salt and freshly ground black pepper

Cheese and Ham Stuffed Mushrooms

1. Preheat the oven to 190°C
   (170°C fan) / 375F / gas 5.

2. Beat together the goats' cheese
   and chopped ham with a little
   seasoning until smooth and creamy.

3. Spoon into the button mushrooms
   and arrange on a baking tray.

4. Drizzle with olive oil before
   roasting for 18–20 minutes until
   the mushrooms are tender and the
   filling is lightly browned on top.

5. Remove from the oven and serve
   with a garnish of coriander.

SERVES: **4**

PREPARATION TIME: **10 MINUTES**

COOKING TIME: **45–55 MINUTES**

INGREDIENTS

1 large butternut squash
8 rashers of streaky bacon
a bunch of thyme sprigs
55 ml / 2 fl. oz / ¼ cup olive oil
1 tbsp balsamic vinegar
salt and freshly ground black pepper

Bacon-wrapped Butternut Squash

1. Preheat the oven to 190°C (170°C fan) / 375F / gas 5.

2. Cut the butternut squash in half using a sharp knife; remove any stringy pulp and seeds before splitting each half into quarters.

3. Wrap a couple of rashers of bacon around the middle of each piece, tucking thyme sprigs between the squash and bacon at the same time.

4. Arrange on a baking tray and drizzle with olive oil and balsamic vinegar, seasoning at the same time.

5. Roast for 45–55 minutes until the flesh is tender and the bacon is crisp.

6. Remove from the oven and leave to stand for a few minutes before serving.

CAKES
AND COOKIES

SERVES: **6–8**

PREPARATION TIME: **15–20 MINUTES**

COOKING TIME: **20–30 MINUTES**

INGREDIENTS

175 g / 6 oz / ¾ cup margarine, softened
175 g / 6 oz / ¾ cup caster (superfine) sugar
1 tsp vanilla extract
a pinch of salt
3 large eggs, beaten
175 g / 6 oz / 1 ¼ cups self-raising flour,
 sifted
250 ml / 9 fl. oz / 1 cup double (heavy) cream
225 g / 8 oz / 1 cup strawberry jam (jelly),
 slightly warmed
2 tbsp icing (confectioners') sugar

Cream and Jam Sponge Cake

1. Preheat the oven to 180°C (160°C fan) / 350F / gas 4. Grease and line the base of two 18 cm (7 in) cake tins with greaseproof paper.

2. Cream together the margarine, sugar, vanilla extract and salt in a large mixing bowl until pale and thick, about 2–3 minutes.

3. Whisk the beaten eggs into the margarine and sugar, little by little, until incorporated.

4. Fold in the flour, in thirds, until you have a smooth batter.

5. Divide between the two cake tins and tap a few times to help settle the batter.

6. Bake for 25–30 minutes until golden and risen; a cake tester inserted into their middles should come out clean.

7. Remove the tins to a wire rack to cool, then carefully turn out.

8. Whip the cream in a large mixing bowl until softly peaked, then spread over the top of one sponge.

9. Spoon over the jam and sit the other sponge on top. Dust the cake with icing sugar just before serving.

MAKES: **12**

PREPARATION TIME: **30 MINUTES**

COOKING TIME: **18–20 MINUTES**

INGREDIENTS

175 g / 6 oz / ¾ cup caster (superfine)
  sugar
175 g / 6 oz / ¾ cup margarine, softened
175 g / 6 oz / 1 ¼ cups self-raising flour,
  sifted
3 large eggs
1 ½ tsp vanilla extract
a pinch of salt
225 g / 8 oz / 2 cups raspberries
75 g / 3 oz / ⅓ cup unsalted butter,
  softened
150 g / 4 oz / ⅔ cup cream cheese,
  softened
125 g / 4 ½ oz / 1 cup icing
  (confectioners') sugar

Raspberry Cupcakes

1. Preheat the oven to 180°C
   (160°C fan) / 350F / gas 4 and line
   a 12-hole cupcake tin with cases.

2. Beat together the sugar, margarine,
   flour, eggs, salt and 1 tsp of vanilla
   extract in a large mixing bowl
   until pale, smooth and creamy.

3. Place a few raspberries in each
   case, then spoon the batter on
   top. Set 12 aside as a garnish.

4. Tap the tin a few times to help settle
   the batter, then bake for 18–22

minutes until golden and risen; they
should feel springy to the touch.

5. Remove to a wire rack to
   cool, then beat together the
   butter and cream cheese in a
   mixing bowl until smooth.

6. Beat in the icing sugar, little
   by little, then beat in the
   remaining vanilla extract.

7. Spoon into a piping bag fitted with a
   straight-sided nozzle.

8. Pipe swirls of icing onto the cupcakes
   and garnish with a raspberry on top.

INGREDIENTS

250 g / 9 oz / 1 ⅔ cups plain (all
   purpose) flour
55 g / 2 oz / ⅓ cup cocoa powder
2 tsp baking powder
2 large eggs
110 g / 4 oz / ½ cup golden caster
   (superfine) sugar
55 ml / 2 fl. oz / ¼ cup vegetable oil
225 ml / 8 fl. oz / 1 cup whole milk
1 tsp vanilla extract
2 tbsp icing (confectioners') sugar

Chocolate Muffins

1. Preheat the oven to 160°C (140°C fan) / 325F / gas 3 and line a 12-hole muffin, or cupcake tray with cases.

2. Sieve the flour, cocoa powder and baking powder into a large mixing bowl.

3. Combine the eggs, sugar, oil, milk and vanilla extract in a large jug and whisk together until combined.

4. Pour into the dry ingredients and stir until just combined; take care to not overmix the batter.

5. Divide the batter between the cases and bake for 20–25 minutes until set and starting to crack on top; test with a wooden toothpick, if it comes out clean, the muffins are done.

6. Remove the muffins to a wire rack to cool.

7. Once cool, dust with icing sugar before serving.

SERVES: **10–12**

PREPARATION TIME: **1 HOUR**

SOAKING TIME: **24 HOURS**

COOKING TIME: **2 HRS 15 MINUTES**

INGREDIENTS

1kg / 2.2 1lbs / 5 cups mixed dried fruits (use a
    mix of raisins, sultanas, diced dried apricots,
    currants, cherries, prunes)
zest and juice 1 orange
zest and juice 1 lemon
150ml / 5 fl. oz / ⅔ cup whiskey
250g / 8 oz / 2 sticks butter, softened
225g / 8 oz / 1 cup Muscavado sugar
175g / 6 oz / 1 ¼ cups plain flour
110g / 4 oz / 1 cup ground almonds
½ tsp baking powder
2 tsp mixed spice
3 tbsp black treacle
1 ½ tsp mixed spice
110g / 4 oz / ¾ cup blanched almonds
4 large free-range eggs
1 tsp vanilla extract

Rich Fruit Cake

1. Put the fruit in a large non-
    metallic bowl. Add the whiskey,
    juice and zest of the orange and
    lemon, cover with cling film and
    leave to marinate for 24 hours.

2. Preheat the oven to 150°C (130°C
    fan) / 300F / gas 2. Grease and line
    a 20cm (8 in) round cake tin with a
    double layer of greaseproof paper.

3. Cream together the butter
    and Muscavado sugar.

4. Gently beat the eggs and add little by
    little to the creamed butter adding a
    spoonful of flour if it starts to curdle.

5. Sift the baking powder, mixed
    spice and flour together and
    add to the wet ingredients.

6. Gradually incorporate the ground
    almonds and black treacle and
    mix thoroughly. Add the fruits and
    vanilla extract into the mixture
    and stir well to combine.

7. Pour the mixture into the cake tin
    and smooth the top with a wet
    spoon making a well in the middle.
    Gently tap the tin against the work-
    surface to remove any air bubbles.

8. Place the blanched almonds

in a decorative way on
the top of the cake.

9. Wrap a double layer of brown paper
    around the tin and secure with string.

10. Place the cake tin onto a double layer
    square of brown paper to prevent
    the bottom of the cake from burning.

11. Cook the cake for 2 hours 15 minutes
    testing with a skewer after 2 hours. If
    it comes out clean the cake is cooked.

12. Leave to cool in the tin, then
    turn out for serving.

SERVES: **6–8**

PREPARATION TIME: **15–20 MINUTES**

COOKING TIME: **40–50 MINUTES**

INGREDIENTS

150 g / 5 oz / ⅔ cup caster (superfine) sugar
150 g / 5 oz / ⅔ cup butter, softened
a little extra butter, for greasing
150 g / 5 oz / 1 cup self-raising flour, sifted
3 small eggs
1 tsp lemon extract
125 g / 4 ½ oz / 1 cup icing (confectioners')
   sugar, sifted
1 lemon, juiced

Iced Lemon Cake

1. Preheat the oven to 160°C (140°C fan) / 325F / gas 3 and grease and line a 20 cm (8 in) springform cake tin with greaseproof paper.

2. Grease the top of the paper with a little butter.

3. Beat together the sugar, butter, flour, eggs and lemon extract in a large mixing bowl until pale, thick and creamy.

4. Spoon into the prepared cake tin and bake for 40–50 minutes until a cake tester inserted into the middle comes out clean.

5. Remove to a wire rack to cool as you prepare the icing.

6. Whisk together the icing sugar and lemon juice in a small saucepan. Cook over a low heat until the icing stars to bubble.

7. Remove from the heat and leave to thicken.

8. Turn out the cake and pour the thickened icing over the top, letting it run over the edges to coat.

9. Slice and serve once the icing has set.

SERVES: **6–8**

PREPARATION TIME: **15 MINUTES**

COOKING TIME: **1 HOUR 10 MINUTES**

INGREDIENTS

125 g / 4 ½ oz / ⅔ cup pitted dates, roughly
   chopped
55 g / 2 oz / ¼ cup margarine, softened
225 ml / 8 fl. oz / 1 cup boiling water
1 tsp bicarbonate of (baking) soda
a pinch of salt
225 g / 8 oz / 1 ½ cups self-raising flour, sifted
175 g / 6 oz / ¾ cup golden caster (superfine)
   sugar
75 g / 3 oz / ⅔ cup walnuts, chopped
1 large egg, beaten

Date and Walnut Cake

1. Preheat the oven to 160°C (140°C fan) / 325F / gas 3. Grease and line a 900 g (2 lb) loaf tin with greaseproof paper on its base and sides.

2. Combine the dates, margarine, water, bicarbonate of soda and salt in a large mixing bowl.

3. Mix well with a wooden spoon, then leave to cool.

4. Combine the flour, sugar and most of the walnuts in a separate bowl and add to the wet ingredients.

5. Mix well and then beat in the egg. Scrape the mixture into the prepared loaf tin and sprinkle over the remaining walnuts.

6. Bake for 1 hour–1 hour 10 minutes, until a cake tester inserted into the middle comes out clean.

7. Remove to a wire rack to cool, then turn out and serve.

SERVES: **8**

PREPARATION TIME: **30–40 MINUTES**

COOKING TIME: **40–50 MINUTES**

INGREDIENTS

450 g / 1 lb / 3 cups dark chocolate, chopped
275 g / 10 oz / 1 ¼ cups unsalted butter, softened
225 g / 8 oz / 1 cup caster (superfine) sugar
1 tsp vanilla extract
8 small eggs, separated
175 g / 6 oz / 1 ¾ cups ground almonds
110 g / 4 oz / ⅔ cup plain (all purpose) flour, sifted
100 g / 3 ½ oz / ½ cup apricot jam (jelly), sieved
175 ml / 6 fl. oz / ¾ cup double (heavy) cream
1 tbsp liquid glucose

Sachertorte

1. Preheat the oven to 180°C (160°C fan) / 350F / gas 4, then grease and line two 20 cm (8 in) springform cake tins with greaseproof paper.

2. Place 300 g of the chocolate in a bain marie set over a saucepan of simmering water. Leave to melt, stirring occasionally.

3. Meanwhile, cream together the butter, sugar and vanilla extract in a separate mixing bowl until pale and creamy. Beat in the cooled chocolate and egg yolks. Fold through the ground almonds and flour until the batter is thick.

4. Beat the egg whites in a large bowl until stiff. Whisk one-third into the batter, then fold through the rest. Divide the batter between the prepared cake tins, ensuring the mix is level, then bake for 40–50 minutes until risen. Place on the wire racks to cool, then turn out once cooled.

5. Cut each sponge horizontally so that you have four rounds. Warm the apricot jam in a small saucepan, then brush over the cakes and leave to set. Combine the remaining chocolate with the liquid glucose in a heatproof bowl. Bring the cream to boiling point, then pour over the chocolate. Leave for 2 minutes and stir until smooth. Leave to cool until it reaches a coating consistency.

6. Spread some of the ganache on top of three rounds of sponge, then stack them together. Place the final sponge round on top and pour the remaining ganache over to coat the top and sides, then slice and serve.

SERVES: **12**

PREPARATION TIME: **15–20 MINUTES**

COOKING TIME: **35–40 MINUTES**

INGREDIENTS

300 g / 10 ½ oz / 2 cups good-quality dark
  chocolate, chopped
225 g / 8 oz / 1 cup unsalted butter, softened
4 large eggs
250 g / 9 oz / 1 ⅓ cups soft light brown sugar
110 g / 4 oz / ⅔ cup plain (all purpose) flour
1 tsp baking powder
a pinch of salt
100 g / 3 ½ oz / ⅔ cup milk chocolate

Classic Brownies

1. Preheat the oven to 170°C (150°C fan) / 325F / gas 3 and grease and line an 18 cm (7 in) square baking tray with greaseproof paper.

2. Melt the chocolate and butter in a saucepan over a medium-low heat, stirring occasionally until smooth.

3. Remove from the heat and leave to cool.

4. In a large mixing bowl, beat the eggs until thick, then add the sugar and continue to beat until glossy.

5. Beat in the melted chocolate mixture and then fold through the flour, baking powder and salt until incorporated.

6. Pour into the baking tray and tap lightly a few times to release any trapped air bubbles.

7. Bake for 35–40 minutes until the surface has set and a cake tester inserted into the middle comes out clean.

8. Remove to a wire rack and leave to cool completely, then turn out and cut into squares.

9. Grate a generous amount of milk chocolate on top before serving.

Royal Icing

MAKES: **350 G / 12 OZ ICING / 1 ½ CUPS**

PREPARATION TIME: **5 MINUTES**

MAKING TIME: **8–10 MINUTES**

250 g / 9 oz / 2 cups icing sugar, sifted
2 medium egg whites
½ tsp glycerine

1. Place the egg whites in a large bowl and stir in the icing sugar, one tablespoon at a time, until thick.

2. Once the icing falls thickly from a spoon, beat with an electric whisk for 8–10 minutes until stiffly peaked.

3. Stir through the glycerine before using.

Buttercream Icing

MAKES: **700 G / 1 LB 12 OZ / 3 ½ CUPS**

PREPARATION TIME: **5 MINUTES**

MAKING TIME: **5–10 MINUTES**

225 g / 8 oz / 1 cup unsalted butter, softened
450 g / 1 lb / 3 ½ cups icing (confectioners') sugar
1 tsp vanilla extract
2–3 tbsp whole milk

1. Beat the butter in a large mixing bowl using an electric hand-held whisk until pale and creamy; 2–3 minutes.

2. Sift over half of the icing sugar and beat, starting slowly at first, until smooth.

3. Sift over the rest of the icing sugar and add the vanilla extract and 1 tbsp of the milk; beat until smooth, adding more milk to loosen if necessary.

4. Once the buttercream is creamy and spreadable, either spoon into a piping bag for piping or spread directly onto cakes.

Cream Cheese Icing

MAKES: **700 G / I LB I2 OZ / 3 ½ CUPS**

PREPARATION TIME: **5 MINUTES**

MAKING TIME: **5 MINUTES**

225 g / 8 oz / I cup unsalted butter, softened
75 g / 3 oz / ⅓ cup caster (superfine) sugar
I tsp vanilla extract
400 g / I4 oz / 2 cups cream cheese, softened

1. Beat together the butter, caster sugar and vanilla extract in a large mixing bowl using an electric hand-held whisk until pale and creamy; 2–3 minutes.

2. Add half of the cream cheese and beat briefly to incorporate before adding the rest.

3. Beat well until smooth and creamy before spooning into a piping bag or spreading over a cake.

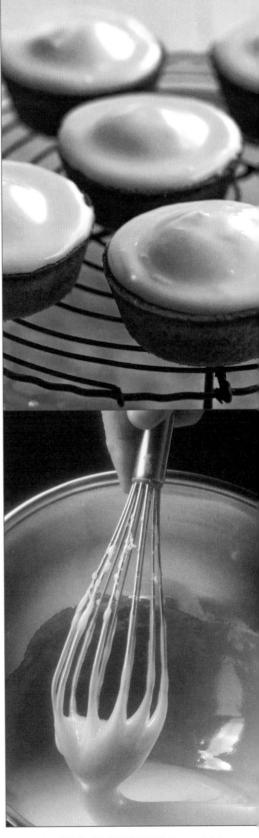

Glace Icing

MAKES: **250 G / 9 OZ / I CUP**

PREPARATION TIME: **5 MINUTES**

MAKING TIME: **5 MINUTES**

250 g / 9 oz / 2 cups icing (confectioners') sugar
55–75 ml / 2–3 fl. oz / ¼–⅓ cup boiling water

1. Sift the icing sugar in a large mixing bowl.

2. Add a tablespoon of the boiling water and whisk carefully and slowly until a smooth icing starts to form.

3. Whisk in more of the boiling water until the icing reaches the desired consistency for pouring, or spreading.

4. If the icing becomes too thin, whisk in a little more icing sugar to thicken.

MAKES: **12–14**

PREPARATION TIME: **25–30 MINUTES**

COOKING TIME: **12–15 MINUTES**

INGREDIENTS

225 g / 8 oz / 1 ½ cups plain (all purpose)
  flour, sifted
110 g / 4 oz / ½ cup caster (superfine) sugar
½ tsp salt
150 g / 5 oz / ⅔ cup unsalted butter, melted
  and cooled slightly
110 g / 4 oz / ⅔ cup dark chocolate chips
2 medium eggs, beaten
½ tsp vanilla extract

Chocolate Chip Cookies

1. Mix together the flour, sugar and
   salt in a large mixing bowl. Beat
   in the melted butter until the
   mixture starts to come together.

2. Add the dark chocolate chips,
   eggs and vanilla extract, then mix
   until a stiff cookie dough forms.

3. Cover the bowl and chill
   for 15 minutes.

4. Grease and line two baking
   sheets with greaseproof paper
   and preheat the oven to 180°C
   (160°C fan) / 350F / gas 4.

5. Take generous tablespoons of
   the chilled dough and drop onto
   the sheets, spaced apart.

6. Press down lightly on the dough
   and bake for 12–15 minutes until
   just set and starting to turn golden.

7. Remove to a wire rack to
   cool, before serving.

MAKES: 12–14

PREPARATION TIME: 25–30 MINUTES

COOKING TIME: 12–15 MINUTES

INGREDIENTS

200 g / 7 oz / 1 ⅓ cups plain (all purpose) flour, sifted

150 g / 5 oz / ⅔ cup golden caster (superfine) sugar

75 g / 3 oz / ½ cup cocoa powder, sifted

½ tsp salt

½ tsp baking powder

150 g / 5 oz / ⅔ cup unsalted butter, melted and cooled slightly

2 tbsp whole milk

2 large eggs, beaten

1 tsp vanilla extract

Chocolate Cookies

1. Mix together the flour, sugar, cocoa powder, salt and baking powder in a large mixing bowl.

2. Beat in the melted butter and milk until the mixture starts to come together.

3. Add the eggs and vanilla extract, then mix until a stiff cookie dough forms.

4. Cover the bowl and chill for 15 minutes. Grease and line two baking sheets with greaseproof paper and preheat the oven to 180°C (160°C fan) / 350F / gas 4.

5. Take generous tablespoons of the chilled dough and drop onto the sheets, spaced apart.

6. Press down lightly on the dough, then bake for 12–15 minutes until just set and starting to crack on top.

7. Remove to a wire rack to cool before serving.

PUDDINGS

Steaming Puddings

Some kinds of puddings, such as Christmas pudding, need to be steamed rather than baked. A batter is spooned into a heatproof pudding bowl, then covered with a layer of greaseproof paper and a sheet of foil. A handle can be fashioned from kitchen string and tied around the rim to secure and make lowering and removing the pudding easier. Once you have covered the pudding, lower it into a saucepan of simmering water. Cover the saucepan with a lid and let the steam cook the batter gently until it is set. The water may need to be topped up with fresh boiling water from time to time, in order to prevent it from drying out. When the pudding is ready, it is removed from the saucepan and left to cool slightly, then turned out and served. Most steamed puddings are great served with thick custard, or a dash of cold cream on the side.

Baking Puddings

For lighter sponge puddings, you can simply bake your batter in an oven. Start by preheating your oven to 180°C (160°C fan) / 350F / gas 4 and grease a baking dish with a little softened butter. Prepare your sponge batter according to recipe. A layer of warmed marmalade, or stewed fruit works well in sponge puddings, so spoon either onto the base of your prepared pudding dish. Top with the sponge batter, smoothing it down with the back of spoon, then bake the pudding for 35–45 minutes until the sponge is golden on top and cooked through. Test the sponge layer with a cake tester; if it comes out clean, the sponge is ready. Remove from the oven and leave to stand for a few minutes before serving with cream, custard, or ice cream as an accompaniment.

Poaching Fruit

Certain varieties of fruit, such as stone fruit, benefit from poaching to soften their flesh and skins before serving. Fruits, such as plums, peaches, apricot, or pears, can be poached in a simple sugar syrup solution, or in simmering wine. For example, bring a bottle of red wine (it doesn't need to be expensive) to the simmer with 100 g / 3 ½ oz / ½ cup sugar, as well as aromatics, such as cinnamon, clove and orange peel. Once the sugar has dissolved, add a couple of large handfuls of halved and stoned plums into the liquid. Leave them to poach in the simmering liquid for 30–40 minutes until very tender. For lighter fruits, such as apricots, you can prepare this recipe using white wine rather than red to help them retain their colour. Poached fruit is an ideal accompaniment to cakes, or served simply with a little vanilla ice cream.

Creams and Mousses

Creams can make an elegant, luxurious accompaniment to desserts, pudding and sweets. Pouring cream is perfect served over fruit crumbles and sponge puddings. Double (heavy) and whipping cream can be whipped until light and airy before spooning atop trifles, or sandwiched between meringues and served with red fruits. For most mousse recipes, whipped cream is a key component; the whipped cream is gently folded together with a meringue-type mixture before being spooned into serving glasses and chilled until ready to serve.

SERVES: **4–6**

PREPARATION TIME: **15–20 MINUTES**

COOKING TIME: **I HR 45 MINUTES**

INGREDIENTS

250 g / 9 oz / 1 ⅔ cups self-raising flour,
  sifted
110 g / 4 oz / ½ cup shredded suet
175 g / 6 oz / 1 ¼ cups currants
110 g / 4 oz / ¼ cup caster (superfine) sugar
1 lemon, finely zested
750 ml / 1 pint 6 fl. oz / 3 cups whole milk
2 tbsp instant custard powder

Spotted Dick

1. Place the flour, suet, currants, three-quarters of the sugar and the lemon zest in a mixing bowl; stir well to combine.

2. Add 150 ml of the milk and mix with a wooden spoon until a moist, even dough comes together; add a little more milk if it seems too dry.

3. Place the dough in a 900 g (2 lb) greased pudding bowl before covering the bowl with a folded round of greaseproof paper and then foil.

4. Tie string around the perimeter of the bowl to secure; place the pudding bowl in a large saucepan.

5. Pour in boiling water so that it comes two-thirds of the way up the side of the pudding bowl.

6. Turn the heat on and bring to a simmer before reducing and covering the saucepan with a lid.

7. Steam for 1 hour 45 minutes, topping up the boiling water as necessary, until the pudding is cooked.

8. Heat the remaining milk in a saucepan until it reaches boiling point; meanwhile, whisk together the custard powder with the remaining sugar and 1–2 tbsp of the milk in a jug to form a smooth paste.

9. Whisk in the hot milk and continue until the custard thickens; serve with the steamed pudding.

SERVES: **6–8**

PREPARATION TIME: **20 MINUTES**

COOKING TIME: **35–40 MINUTES**

INGREDIENTS

150 g / 5 oz / 1 ½ cups chocolate digestive
   biscuits
1 tbsp cocoa powder
75 g / 3 oz / ⅓ cup unsalted butter, melted
300 g / 10 ½ oz / 1 cup golden syrup, warmed
150 g / 5 oz / ½ cup treacle, warmed
100 g / 3 ½ oz / 1 ¼ cups fresh breadcrumbs
75 g / 3 oz / ½ cup dark chocolate, broken
vanilla ice cream, to serve

Treacle Tart

1. Preheat the oven to 180°C (160°C fan) / 350F / gas 4.

2. Pulse the biscuits in a food processor until finely ground. Add the cocoa powder and melted butter and pulse again until the mixture resembles wet sand.

3. Scrape the mixture into a 20 cm (8 in) springform pie dish, or tart case, pressing well into the base and sides using the back of a tablespoon. Chill for 15 minutes.

4. Mix together the golden syrup, treacle and breadcrumbs in a large mixing bowl, then pour into the chilled pie dish.

5. Bake for 35–40 minutes until set. Remove from the oven and leave to cool on a wire rack.

6. Once cool, turn out and arrange on a serving plate.

7. Melt the chocolate in a heatproof bowl set over a saucepan of simmering water, stirring until smooth. Leave to cool for 5 minutes, then drizzle over the tart.

8. Leave the chocolate to set before slicing and serving with vanilla ice cream.

SERVES: **6–8**

PREPARATION TIME: **30–35 MINUTES**

COOKING TIME: **45–50 MINUTES**

INGREDIENTS

150 g / 5 oz / 1 cup strawberries, hulled and halved
110 g / 4 oz / 1 cup raspberries
110 g / 4 oz / 1 cup blueberries
2 tbsp granulated sugar
½ lemon, juiced
110 g / 4 oz / ⅔ cup digestive biscuits
55 g / 2 oz / ¼ cup unsalted butter
600 g / 1 lb 5 oz / 3 cups cream cheese
150 g / 5 oz / ⅔ cup golden caster (superfine) sugar
2 tbsp plain (all purpose) flour
100 g / 3 ½ oz / ½ cup soured cream
2 tsp vanilla extract
2 large eggs, 1 large egg yolk
a few sprigs of mint leaves

Cheesecake with Fruit Purée

1. Combine most of the strawberries, raspberries and blueberries in a saucepan with the granulated sugar, then cook over a low heat until softened and juicy.

2. Purée in a food processor before straining into a bowl. Adjust to taste using lemon juice, then cover and chill until needed.

3. Preheat the oven to 160°C (140°C fan) / 300F / gas 2.

4. Crush the digestives, melt the butter and mix together in a bowl, then pack into the base and sides of a 18 cm (7 in) springform cake tin and chill.

5. Beat together the cream cheese, golden caster sugar and flour until smooth, then continue to beat in the soured cream, vanilla extract, eggs and egg yolk.

6. Pour half into the cake tin and spoon over a little of the fruit purée.

7. Pour over the remaining mixture and sit the tin in a baking tray half-filled with hot water.

8. Bake for 45–50 minutes until a knife comes out clean from the middle. Spoon over more of the purée and return the cheesecake to the oven for a few minutes.

9. Turn off the oven, crack the door and leave it to cool. Cover and chill in the fridge.

10. Once chilled, remove the cheesecake from the fridge and cut into slices using a hot, wet knife.

11. Serve with the reserved fruit, fruit purée and a sprig of mint.

SERVES: **4**

PREPARATION TIME: **25 MINUTES**

COOKING TIME: **35–45 MINUTES**

INGREDIENTS

250 ml / 9 fl. oz / 1 cup whole milk
250 ml / 9 fl. oz / 1 cup double (heavy) cream
1 tsp vanilla extract
6 large egg yolks
75 g / 3 oz / ⅓ cup caster (superfine) sugar
75 g / 3 oz / ⅓ cup stem ginger in syrup, finely chopped
2 tbsp granulated sugar

Ginger Crème Brûlée

1. Preheat the oven to 150°C (130°C fan) / 300F / gas 2.

2. Combine the milk, cream and vanilla extract in a saucepan. Bring to a simmer over a moderate heat.

3. Whisk together the egg yolks, sugar and 2 tbsp of the ginger syrup in a large mixing bowl until pale and thick.

4. Pour the milk and cream on top in a slow, steady stream, whisking simultaneously until smooth.

5. Drain the mixture into a jug and pour into 4 individual ramekins.

6. Place the ramekins in a roasting tray and fill with boiling water so that it reaches halfway up the sides of the ramekins.

7. Bake for 35–45 minutes until set at the edges but with a slight wobble in the middle.

8. Remove from the oven and leave to cool for a few minutes before topping with granulated sugar.

9. Caramelise the sugar using a chef's blowtorch, or under a hot grill. Leave to cool and set.

10. Spoon a little chopped ginger and syrup on top before serving.

SERVES: **4**

PREPARATION TIME: **15–20 MINUTES**

COOKING TIME: **45–50 MINUTES**

INGREDIENTS

4 large ripe pears
1.5 l / 2 pints 12 fl. oz / 6 cups cold water
110 g / 4 oz / ½ cup caster (superfine) sugar
1 tsp vanilla extract
200 g / 7 oz / 1 ⅓ cups dark chocolate,
   chopped
2 tbsp unsalted butter, chopped
1 tbsp golden syrup
vanilla ice cream, to serve

Pears with Chocolate Sauce

1. Peel the pears using a vegetable peeler, leaving their stalks intact.

2. Combine the water, sugar and vanilla extract in a saucepan and bring to a simmer, stirring to help dissolve the sugar.

3. Place the pears in the simmering liquid and cover with a round of greaseproof paper on top.

4. Leave them to poach over a low heat for 45–50 minutes until tender.

5. Remove the pears from the liquid once ready and set to one side to cool.

6. Melt together the chocolate, butter and golden syrup in a heatproof bowl set over a saucepan of simmering water.

7. Remove from the heat and stir briefly until smooth. Leave to cool and thicken for 5 minutes.

8. Place the pears in bowls and top with the chocolate sauce and serve with scoops of vanilla ice cream.

SERVES: **4**

PREPARATION TIME: **2 HRS 20 MINUTES**

COOKING TIME: **5 MINUTES**

INGREDIENTS

2 tbsp unsalted butter
100 g / 3 ½ oz / ⅔ cup dark chocolate, chopped
3 medium eggs, separated
½ tsp vanilla extract
2 tbsp caster (superfine) sugar
a pinch of salt
1 dark chocolate flake, crushed

Chocolate Mousse

1. Combine the butter and chopped chocolate in a heatproof bowl set over a saucepan of simmering water.

2. Leave to melt, then stir until smooth. Remove from the heat and leave to cool slightly.

3. Beat together the egg yolks, vanilla extract and caster sugar in a bowl until pale and thick.

4. Fold this mixture into the cooled chocolate until well combined.

5. Whisk the egg whites with a pinch of salt in a large, clean bowl until stiffly peaked.

6. Fold the egg whites into the chocolate mixture, working gently, but thoroughly before spooning the mixture into 4 individual serving cups.

7. Chill for at least 2 hours before serving with flaked chocolate on top.

How-to Index

Recipe Index

Recipe Index